MILLENNIUM
MONOLOGS

95 contemporary charac ors

EDITED BY

GERALD LEE RATLIFF

Meriwether Publishing Ltd., Publisher
PO Box 7710
Colorado Springs, CO 80933-7710

Executive editor: Theodore O. Zapel
Cover design: Janice Melvin

Library of Congress Cataloging-in-Publication Data

Millennium monologs : 95 contemporary characterizations for
    young actors / edited by Gerald Lee Ratliff -- 1st ed.
      p. cm.
    Summary: An anthology of monologues by contemporary writers,
    divided into four categories; "Hope and Longing," "Spirit and
    Soul," "Fun and Fantasy," and "Doubt and Despair." Includes
    audition techniques.
    ISBN 1-56608-082-7
    1. Monologues. 2. Acting. 3. American drama--20th century.
    [1. Monologues. 2. Acting. 3. American drama--20th century.]
    I. Ratliff, Gerald Lee.
    PN2080.M44 2002
    792'.028'02373--dc21

2002013009

1   2   3   02   03   04

Contents

Introduction

"Acting is ... forever carving a statue of snow."
Lawrence Barrett

This collection of millennium monologs features familiar, well-established authors who voice traditional views on current issues and a host of new, contemporary authors who offer fresh, original insights on similar topics. The themes dramatized here are emotionally sensitive and intellectually challenging, encouraging a keen and discerning insight in performance. Many of the authors address fundamental issues of life and death, love and loss, or hope and despair. Other more adventurous authors address controversial issues of suicide, brutality, and social injustice.

The book is divided into "voices" rather than standard categories that identify characters simply by age, gender, and point of view. The individual voices express themes like hope and longing, spirit and soul, fantasy and fun, or despair and doubt. Look at each voice section for a list of monologs that represent the selected theme. Each section also concludes with a "multiple" voice performance script that is appropriate for group work or small ensemble role-playing.

Performance roles are generally indicated as female (F) or male (M). A number of roles, with some modification, may also be played by either female or male actors and are indicated as (M/F). You might want to thumb through the "Table of Contents" to get a sense of the female, male, or male/female roles available. Or, if you have initial questions about a character's age, gender, or type go directly to the brief introduction of each script for author comments or performance suggestions. You may also need to edit some of the longer monolog selections to meet audition or classroom performance time limits.

The Audition Process

Before choosing a promising monolog for performance, you need to understand the audition process. The first type of audition is the "cold reading," where you are given a prepared speech and asked to perform with little or no time for preparation. Some directors use the cold reading to evaluate initial skills in interpretation, phrasing, vocal range, and physical type. The cold reading may also include impromptu vocal or physical exercises suggested by the director.

1

The second type of audition is the "prepared reading," where you are asked to perform two brief monologs — usually contrasting ones — of two minutes each from classical, Shakespeare, modern, or contemporary scripts. Most directors use the prepared reading to evaluate an actor's ability to clearly distinguish different character attitudes or moods. Some directors use the prepared reading to catalogue actor "types" for later callbacks. Other directors use the prepared reading to determine a general level of potential talent available before pursuing a specific production concept.

There may be "open" auditions that encourage all actors to attend. Auditions may also be "closed," and only actors who have been invited may attend. "General" auditions are most common and used to screen actors for more intensive review at later, more structured audition sessions. Auditions frequently feature improvisations designed to challenge an actor's imagination in a series of impromptu vocal and physical exercises. There are also "directed readings," where the director may give specific instructions in movement or interpretation and then evaluate an actor's ability to follow directions while exhibiting a degree of risk-taking.

Remember, however, that honesty and simplicity are the essential ingredients of success for all audition situations. Approach the audition in a calm, relaxed manner so a true-to-life performance emerges. Think of the monolog performance as a current event or recent happening simply being dramatized. Directors are especially interested in the "spirit" of the character you are performing, so be spontaneous, living and responding moment-to-moment in your character's brief audition life.

An audition is similar to an interview for a job — only in the audition you are "performing" answers to the questions asked by the director. A successful audition involves much more than just a basic appreciation and understanding of performance technique. There must also be careful analysis of the script and rehearsal to discover the clues needed to sketch a memorable character portrait. It is also important to avoid overly precise use of the voice, exaggerated movement, or theatrical posing in an audition.

Basic Audition Principles

There are a number of basic principles to consider when preparing for an audition. For example, it is important to be adaptable and flexible in the audition. Being adaptable and flexible suggests that you (1) maintain a repertoire of several monologs that serve any type of audition call (2) prepare for the audition by reading the entire script, not just the monolog excerpt (3) pay particular attention to audition monologs that promote vocal variety, ease of movement, and emotional honesty.

Please review the following basic audition principles before selecting any monolog for performance. This does not mean that you need to select a monolog that matches "you" identically in age, gender, or race. It is more important that you understand the character and can relate to the experience expressed in the monolog.

- Auditions are generally limited to three or four minutes for two contrasting monologs. Edit long scripts to meet the time limit.

- Auditions that specifically call for a "classical" selection mean a script written in verse.

- Auditions are in Standard American speech that is free of vocal regionalism, colloquialism, or distracting speech patterns. The use of accents should be limited and then only if authentic.

- Auditions start on time and monologs are memorized.

- Auditions may require an interview or resume review so be prepared.

- Auditions cause anxiety so avoid sugar and caffeine in the hours before your call. Don't chew gum during an audition!

You also need to anticipate the initial "stage fright" that accompanies auditions and other performance situations like speaking, dancing, or singing. We all experience the basic symptoms of stage fright before an audition. Stage fright usually reveals itself in a feeling of anxiety and nervousness that affects the voice and the body. With experience, and a positive attitude, you will learn how to cope with the sweaty palms, knocking knees, and pounding heart that are symptoms of stage fright.

A good starting point is to consider every performance situation as an opportunity to develop confidence and relaxation skills. Actively seek to participate in performance activities — oral reports, small group discussions, social meetings — that cultivate a relaxed voice and a body that is tension-free. The more you actively participate in performance activities, the easier it will be to exhibit a comfortable portrait of poise in an audition.

Standard Audition Etiquette

There is a standard audition "etiquette" that you should practice to enhance your competitive edge. For instance, it may not be a good idea to select a monolog from a script you have recently performed. Once you take the monolog out of context, it may not accurately reveal the character's attitude or mood as it was developed in depth within the full-length script. The first twenty-five seconds of a monolog may be the most important in terms of demonstrating your potential range of emotional, physical, and vocal qualities. The last twenty-five seconds of a monolog may also be important to show character development through subtle shifts in gesture, posture, voice, and movement.

In order to familiarize yourself with some of the special features of standard audition etiquette, please review the following practices and incorporate them in your audition blueprint. Although you will probably learn more about audition etiquette through actual experience, the following principles should guide you in constructing a rehearsal routine that showcases your talents. Remember that it is seldom easy in an audition to overcome the fact that you are basically an actor performing in an empty space. That is why it is important to create the illusion that you are living within the "stage world" of the monolog character rather than acting in an empty room or on a bare stage.

Introduction

The first step in putting the audition together is to introduce yourself and the monolog(s) you are performing. Don't think of the introduction as a "non-performance" moment. It is your first entrance on stage and should be marked with a personal signature of self-confidence. The spoken introduction should be brief, efficient, and cordial. A sample introduction might simply say, "Hello. My name is_____. I'll be doing monologs from Tennessee Williams' *The Glass Menagerie*' and Paula Vogel's *The Baltimore Waltz*." Don't forget to pause between the end of the introduction and the beginning of the transition that sets the scene.

Transition(s)

After deciding the order in which to perform your monologs, use brief transitions to move easily from one to the other. Of course, if you are only performing one monolog then there is only one transition necessary to set the scene. Transition statements should be memorized and generally include brief remarks that identify the character, the setting, and the situation. A sample transition for Tennessee Williams'

The Glass Menagerie, for example, might include this description: "Tom, a young man disillusioned with his dead-end shoe salesman job, sits on a fire-escape railing late at night and imagines himself in a more adventurous world of intrigue and mystery."

Time

Anticipate arriving early for an audition — and never arrive late! The audition time is an appointment and you must be punctual. Although the old theatre slogan "Hurry up ... and wait your turn!" remains in practice for auditions, you can review your monolog(s) or warm-up with vocal and physical exercises while waiting to have your name called. Avoid the tendency to socialize at an audition, and show respect for fellow actors by keeping conversation and noise to a minimum. Time also refers to the minutes allocated for individual auditions — so respect the time limits set for each actor. As you rehearse, it may be necessary to time your monolog and make appropriate cuts to meet the announced time limit.

Wardrobe

An appropriate audition wardrobe subtly reflects the attitude or mood of the character. The wardrobe should be carefully selected in terms of cut, style, and color to enhance your physical dimensions. Avoid the tendency to wear theatrical costumes to an audition and focus on traditional designer principles of line, color, texture, and simple ornament. Do not wear hose just because you're playing Shakespeare! Wearing comfortable clothes and shoes that permit easy, fluid movement is always a good idea. Remember that your audition wardrobe can also reveal your character's idiosyncrasies, life style, occupation, or sense of self.

Make-up

Light street make-up is appropriate for women and a warm bronzer for men. Women sometimes wear their hair up for classical monologs but always away from the face so expressions may be clearly seen. Men sometimes experiment with growing mustaches, sideburns, or period hairstyles. If you have long hair, pull it back so it doesn't fall in your face while you are performing! Do not rely on elaborate accessories such as wigs, hair extensions, or prosthetic devices that might be distracting. You should also avoid wearing platform shoes, flip-flops, or high-heels that tend to make movement awkward and unnatural.

Props

Props should be limited to those specific "objects" that are an essential extension of your audition character (like Captain Queeg's marbles in *The Caine Mutiny* or Sister Rita's rosary in *The Runner Stumbles*). If you choose to use a prop, it should be clearly indicated in the script and small enough to be handled easily. Do not litter the stage with an assortment of props or objects that later become part of your performance. Neglect of a well-prepared and carefully rehearsed use of props usually results in an audition that appears disorganized. Remember that an audition is never about props or other theatrical accessories. An audition is about you and how you fill an empty space using yourself as a prop!

Space

You should visit the audition space before a scheduled appointment day. Pay particular attention to the size of the space, entrance and exit doorways, seating arrangement, and acoustical sound. If possible, rehearse in the space to discover the vocal and physical demands of the playing area. Familiarity with the space should help promote a more relaxed atmosphere in which to execute fluid, natural movement and promote an attractive vocal quality in performance. Rehearsal in the space should also help to combat the initial anxiety and tension frequently associated with performing in an unfamiliar environment.

Movement

Although movement plays a significant role in fleshing out character development in the full-length script, it is less likely to have an immediate impact on an abbreviated audition. Expressive movement, however, is an expectation in the audition, and you should explore subtle movement opportunities that help define your character portrait in terms of stance, posture, and gesture. Character intention or motivation can be simply revealed by the manner in which a character sits, walks, or stands. The degree of movement in an audition is always relative. A good rule of thumb is to maintain a balance between movement that helps to visualize the character's action and movement that adds variety to the tempo of the audition performance.

Staging

The only furniture you will probably have available to you in an audition is a chair! It is not necessary to use assorted tables, sofas, beds, or other elaborate set pieces in staging a monolog. What is important is "placement" in the space. Set up the space so you are facing the audience, but place your character at a smart angle downstage. Be careful not to deliver the entire monolog in profile. Look for opportunities to address the audience directly, full-front. Unless you have a specific reason to do otherwise, stage the monolog in the center of the playing space and move downstage or left/right as the monolog continues. Backing up or turning around and moving upstage may suggest that you are retreating or starting over.

Audience

It takes a measure of discipline and self-confidence to perform solo in front of an audience. Do not lose your concentration or focus if individual members of the audience suddenly look down to write or turn to whisper to each other. They may actually be writing positive comments or sharing favorable opinions on your audition skills. It may be a good idea not to use a specific individual in the audience to represent the person your character may be addressing. This approach may be very uncomfortable for individual audience members, but may also be distracting for the actor if the focal person should become disinterested and stop paying attention to the performance!

Entrance/Exit

Both an entrance and an exit are part of the audition and need to be handled with poise. As soon as you enter, seize the space! Walk with self-confidence and make direct eye-contact with the audience. If you need to move a chair or set up the space, do so quickly and quietly. Then go directly to the space you have chosen to introduce yourself. Don't forget to pause before and after your introduction. At the end of your audition, pause again to hold the climactic moment of the monolog. Then simply say, "Thank you" and exit with the same poise that marked your entrance. Do not comment on your performance — especially to offer apologies or make excuses. Be prepared if you are asked to do a cold reading or an improvisation following the audition!

Audition Form

The audition form, or try-out sheet, needs to be filled in clearly and completely. It is especially important to indicate both home and work telephone numbers. Don't forget to list all potential conflicts, work hours, regularly scheduled appointments, classes, or any pending obligations that might occur during the rehearsal, production, or performance dates. You should also make mention of any musical instruments played or novelty skills like magic tricks, gymnastics, tap dance, or impersonations. The audition form is similar to a job application form — so suit your response to the specific request and be direct and honest in your description.

Additional Audition Dimensions

There are a number of additional audition dimensions to consider from both the director's and actor's points of view. From the director's point of view, the audition is an opportunity to discover actors who are at ease in the interpretation of the roles they are playing. The director is interested in actors who can demonstrate flexibility in voice/body, sound natural or conversational in the delivery of dialog, and convey a mature intellectual or emotional range of character understanding. The director is also interested in actors who exhibit spontaneity and stage presence.

The director may use an audition to look for compatible pairs of actors — either in terms of contrasts or similarities — as well as the "spark" of an ensemble in making final casting decisions. The director's point of view may also include typecasting or casting against type. Typecasting is selecting actors whose age, height, weight, ethnicity, physique, or personality most clearly resemble the director's own interpretation of the character roles. Casting against type is selecting actors whose size, age, physical appearance, or vocal quality are the exact opposite of what a character role appears to be at first glance.

Recently, there has been a movement toward non-traditional casting and a number of directors now look for actors to play roles which, in past theatre practice, may not have been considered appropriate. Non-traditional casting is color-blind, with no preference given to race, gender, or ethnicity. Non-traditional casting may be conceptual and the director changes the race, gender, or ethnicity of a character to suggest a new interpretation. Non-traditional casting also presents new acting opportunities for trained or untrained actors who are physically challenged in hearing, seeing, speaking, or moving capabilities.

From the actor's point of view, the audition includes additional dimensions like professional photographs or a resume. Professional photographs are 8" x 10" black-and-white head shots. Head shots reveal the actor in an informal, natural pose that is well-lit with limited shadowing. The resume, a thumbnail autobiographical sketch, is also 8" x 10" and should be stapled or attached with rubber cement to the backside of the professional photograph. Essential resume information includes your complete name and mailing address; home and business telephone number; height, weight and age; color of eyes and hair; and vocal singing range.

A professional resume should indicate an actor's previous acting experience and list specific categories that include the name of the character role played, name of the script, name of the theatre, and date of the performance. In listing previous experience, the most current credits are placed first (high school, college/university, community or professional). It is important that the resume include special reference to individual skills or professional training like foreign languages spoken, mime, modern dance, juggling, or sports.

The professional photograph and resume are also part of an actor's audition preparation. Be as careful and conscientious in the preparation of these supporting materials as you are in the time spent in the audition rehearsal. Make sure that all supporting materials are high quality, free of grammatical and typographical errors, and neatly printed on bonded paper or photocopied. Remember that the director's first impression of an actor may not be the audition. It may be a review of the professional photograph and resume submitted before the audition!

Audition Mechanics

Before selecting a final audition script, use a wristwatch with a second hand to time your monolog. Don't forget to allow time for a brief introduction, pauses, transitions, and the build to a climax. Learn to isolate and identify significant images or evocative language that gives your character's dialog its expressive meaning. Use a dictionary to paraphrase the monolog dialog into conversational words and try to reduce the character's thoughts, ideas, and actions to one-word nouns or verbs that can be explored vocally and physically in the rehearsal period. Try to invent a brief, imaginary biography that gives added dimension to your character portrait.

Callbacks

When callbacks are posted the final audition materials are usually chosen for you. Be prepared for vocal or physical improvisations, cold readings, and perhaps, a brief interview session with the director. Try not to plan any responses or reactions in advance. Do not anticipate the character or the scene that you may be asked to perform. It may be a good idea to wear the same audition wardrobe to callbacks in order to refresh the director's memory. Always be attentive to the callback order of scheduled auditions. Know who you follow so that last-minute emergencies like a missing button, drink of water, or restroom pause will not distract your concentration.

Warm-Up

Arrive at an audition at least forty-five minutes in advance and don't forget to warm-up your voice and body! A popular audition warm-up is to relax by lying flat on your back and breathing deeply. Place your hand just above your waistline and begin to inhale/exhale slowly. Notice how the abdominal wall moves in-and-out as your breathing is consciously controlled. After several minutes, stand up and repeat the exercise. Keep your hand at your waist to detect any change in the center of breathing and recite favorite song lyrics. Encourage your diaphragm to expand and contract with a comfortable rhythm. Concentrate on keeping the upper chest from rising and falling. Repeat this exercise for several short periods before the audition and the results should be noticeable!

Going Up

Don't be concerned about "going up," forgetting your lines, during the audition! If you do forget your lines, "just go on!" You should be prepared through the rehearsal period to paraphrase or to improvise the monolog. You are the only person with a complete copy of the audition script — so learn to go on as if any momentary lapse is just an integral part of your performance. Of course, you can reduce the possibility of lapses with regularly scheduled line reading rehearsals that focus on good memorization skills. It is also a good idea to review your dialog aloud — in an isolated room or hallway — rather than silently.

The Rehearsal Blueprint

Preparing for an audition involves much more than just an understanding of performance technique. It includes a rigorous rehearsal period that presents risk-free opportunities to experiment with your script. The rehearsal period is like a creative laboratory that stimulates you to discover new performance insights. It is a time to explore character interpretation and visualize the action and the situation described in the script. It is a time to fill in the blanks left unanswered in the script — especially if there are unresolved questions about character intention or motivation.

Although the rehearsal period is focused on sketching a preliminary character portrait — mannerisms, gestures, movements, and vocal qualities — it is also a time to experiment. Some actors use rehearsal as a time to search for a metaphor — an implied comparison between the character and something inventive — that might give added dimension to character interpretation. Other actors use the rehearsal period to engage in "word play" with lines of dialog to punctuate the language spoken by a character. A few actors use rehearsal to visualize images suggested in the script and to translate those images into character movement.

Regardless of the approach you choose to take in the rehearsal period, there are a number of principles that should inform your choice. Here is a working blueprint to help you design your own rehearsal period.

- Rehearsal should break down the script into a series of character intentions called "beats." A beat begins when a character's intention begins and ends with its completion.

- Rehearsal should encourage an "inner monolog," what the actor is thinking as the character is speaking. The inner monolog is similar to subtext, the hidden meaning of a character's language.

- Rehearsal should permit time to videotape or tape record the script for initial assessment of vocal sound and physical movement.

- Rehearsal should encourage experiments with traditional performance techniques. One familiar technique is Stanislavski's use of "objective memory." This technique asks the actor to recall the basic stimuli present during a past emotional incident and then to re-experience the stimuli in an interpretation of a similar experience described in the script.

- Rehearsal should also encourage experiments with non-traditional performance techniques. One popular alternative technique is "transfer," in which the actor uses a specific reference person from a recent life experience and projects that person's personality onto the character described in the script.

The rehearsal period is the time to begin regularly scheduled sessions in vocal and physical exercise as well. A rehearsal routine that regularly tunes the voice/body helps combat the initial anxiety associated with auditions. Regular exercise in the rehearsal period is essential to condition the voice and body to respond promptly to any vocal or physical audition demand. Regular exercise should help you discover expressive vocal qualities or movement styles that give vitality to your character portrait.

A final suggestion for rehearsal is to preview your audition performance. The invited audience might include friends, roommates, or fellow actors. The primary goal of the preview is to get an initial reaction or response from a live audience. The preview provides an opportunity to make character or interpretation adjustments without seriously compromising what has been discovered in the rehearsal period. The performance awareness that emerges from a preview is invaluable when you need immediate feedback on the clarity of your character portrait.

At this point you should have a good sense of the audition process, basic audition principles, standard audition etiquette, and a working blueprint for the rehearsal period. It is now time to review the monologs you might select for an audition. The scripts that follow feature distinct character voices isolated in a moment of time, place, and action. Each voice is an intimate, fleeting glance at a figure whose brief time on stage forges a unique character portrait. Your ability to embrace these characters and voice their concerns should inspire an authentic and highly personal audition performance.

Voices of Hope and Longing

Voices of Hope and Longing

The voices of hope and longing expressed in these scripts present reality-based moments for an audition. The characters are common men, women, and young adults who express universal human qualities. The scripts are concerned with the emotional turmoil taking place in each character's struggle to express an inner truth related to a personal desire or dream. Probing beneath the surface of each character's life, you will discover inner conflicts, hidden desires, and frustrated passions that provide the dramatic inspiration for an audition.

At first, it may be a challenge to imagine yourself as some of these characters. It may also be a challenge to relate to the basic impulses or spontaneous outbursts of some of these characters. Let the characters speak and listen to their emphatic pleas. Look for subtle performance clues hidden in the dialog to help you design an audition performance blueprint. It may be useful to consider the role that stage business, like handling small props, might play in helping to define the characters as well. Remember to pay special attention to the possible role that behavior, environment, or heredity may have played in shaping each character's voice of hope and longing.

The Last Yankee
by Arthur Miller

1   Patricia — mid forties   Female
2
3   *(Patricia Hamilton, a woman in her mid forties, is clinically*
4   *depressed and has recently been confined to a hospital for*
5   *treatment of drug addiction. Her depression stems from a*
6   *personal sense of failure and resentment of her husband, a*
7   *descendant of one of the nation's Founding Fathers. In this*
8   *scene, Patricia shares her anger with another patient.)*
9
10 I just don't know whether to tell him yet. *(Karen: What?)*
11 That I'm off everything. *(Karen: But he'll like that, won't*
12 *he?)* Oh, yes. But he's going to be doubtful. Which I am,
13 too. Let's face it — I've been on one medication or
14 another for almost twenty years. But I do feel a
15 thousand per cent better. And I really have no idea how
16 it happened. *(Shakes her head.)* Dear God, when I think
17 of him hanging-in there all these years ... I'm so
18 ashamed. But at the same time he's absolutely refused
19 to make any money. Every one of our children has had
20 to work since they could practically write their names. I
21 can't be expected to applaud, exactly. *(Presses her eyes.)*
22 I guess sooner or later you just have to stand up and
23 say, 'I'm normal, I made it.' But it's like standing on top
24 of a stairs and there's no stairs. *(Staring ahead.)* I'll tell
25 you the truth, dear — I've put him through hell and I
26 know it ... *(Tears threaten her.)* I know I have to stop
27 blaming him; it came to me like a vision two weeks ago.
28 I-must-not-blame-Leroy-anymore. And it's amazing, I
29 lost all desire for medication. I could feel it leaving me

1   like a ... like a ghost. *(Slight pause.)* It's just that he's
2   got really well-to-do relatives and he simply will not
3   accept anyone's help. I mean you take the Jews, the
4   Italians, Irish — they've got their Italian-Americans,
5   Irish-Americans, Hispanic-Americans — . They stick
6   together and help each other. But you ever hear of
7   Yankee-Americans? Not on your life. Raise his taxes, rob
8   him blind, the Yankee'll just sit there all alone getting
9   sadder and sadder. But I'm not going to think about it
10   anymore.
11
12
13
14
15
16
17
18
19
20
21
22
23
24
25
26
27
28
29
30
31
32
33
34
35

I Hate Hamlet
by Paul Rudnick

1   Andrew — late twenties   Male

2

3   *(Andrew Rally, a television star in his late twenties, is*

4   *haunted by the ghost of renowned actor John Barrymore. The*

5   *ghost has persuaded Andrew to play the role of Hamlet in a*

6   *Central Park production. Now, sitting alone in his New York*

7   *apartment after his disastrous performance the previous*

8   *evening, Andrew becomes extremely passionate and*

9   *animated as he reflects on the experience.)*

10

11   Last night, right from the start, I knew I was bombing.

12   I sounded big and phony, real thee and thou, and then I

13   started rushing it. Hi, what's new in Denmark? I just

14   could not connect. I couldn't get ahold of it. And while

15   I'm ... babbling, I look out, and there's this guy in the

16   second row, a kid, like 16, obviously dragged there. And

17   he's yawning and he's jiggling his legs and reading his

18   program. And I just wanted to say, hey kid, I'm with

19   you. I can't stand this either! But I couldn't do that, so

20   I just keep feeling worse and worse, just drowning. And

21   I thought, okay, all my questions are answered — I'm

22   not Hamlet, I'm no actor, what am I doing here? And

23   then I get to the soliloquy, the big job. I'm right in the

24   headlights, and I just thought, oh Christ, the hell with

25   it, just do it!

26   To be or not to be, that is the question;

27   Whether 'tis nobler in the mind to suffer

28   The slings and arrows of outrageous fortune,

29   Or to take arms against a sea of troubles

1   And by opposing, end them.
2   And I kept going. I finished the speech, and I look out,
3   and there's the kid — and he's listening. The whole
4   audience — complete silence, total focus. And I was
5   Hamlet. And it lasted about ten more seconds, and then
6   I was back in Hell. And I stayed there. But for that one
7   little bit, for that one speech — I got it. I had it. Hamlet.
8   And only eight thousand lines left to go.
9
10
11
12
13
14
15
16
17
18
19
20
21
22
23
24
25
26
27
28
29
30
31
32
33
34
35

A Flower or Something
by Jolene Goldenthal

1   Mattie — mid to late twenties   Female

2

3   *(Mattie, a woman in her mid to late twenties, has just broken*

4   *up with her boyfriend and is resolved to be more assertive in*

5   *her new role as an independent woman. Here, the free-*

6   *spirited Mattie reflects on her recent past and reveals a most*

7   *unusual and unique hobby. Determined to get on with her*

8   *life, she announces that she is embarking on a journey of*

9   *self-discovery.)*

10

11   **I've got something everybody wants. I'm not kidding.**

12   **You look at me and you go 'What?' Which only shows**

13   **you don't know beans.** *(She waggles her fingers in an*

14   *exaggerated gesture.)* **There's nobody got what I've got.**

15   **Honest. I'm going into the book. I was just like anybody**

16   **else. Honest. Then it happened. I got dumped. This guy**

17   **I thought was so great. Answer to my prayers and all.**

18   **Well, okay. I've been dumped before. But this time I get**

19   **dumped one night and the next morning, the very next**

20   **morning ... Are you ready for this? The very next**

21   **morning I get fired.** *(Pause.)* **Well. That was a bit much.**

22   **I sat down and I thought about it. I had nothing but**

23   **time, right? I came up with the idea that what I need is**

24   **something to make me different. Like outstanding. No**

25   **guy is going to dump me like I am Ms. Nobody. And no**

26   **boss is going to fire me if I don't want to be fired.**

27   *(Raising her hand.)* **So I think 'What?' Miss America I'm**

28   **not. So that's out. I figure maybe shave my head. But I**

29   **don't know. I'm kind of attached to my hair. Get a**

1   motorcycle? Zoom around? Mucho bucks. Let that go. I
2   keep on thinking and then it comes to me. Nails. Really
3   long nails. Everybody wants them. It's a business
4   f'Chrissake. Those dinky little plastic fakes. Paste them
5   on, ruins your nails underneath. So that's when it came
6   to me. Really long nails. All I had to do was wait. No
7   cost. Nothing.
8   So I think like one hand. Let them grow on one hand,
9   keep the other hand short. So I do it. And they grow like
10   crazy. So by now I'm getting some attention. I've got
11   people, strangers, asking me 'How're the nails today?'
12   And I begin to worry, you know. I mean I've been lucky.
13   But still ... Maybe I'm supposed to put some kind of
14   cream on them or something. Maybe eat something
15   special. Forget it. They grow. They grow so one of them
16   curls itself around another one and another one and I tell
17   you, it is some sight.
18   At night sometimes when I'm not doing anything, say
19   maybe it's a tummy going ouch on the tube, or one of
20   those headache things, I stretch out my hand. I hold it
21   near the light and it looks like something. A flower or
22   something. Or curly fries, maybe. I figure I'm ready for
23   the book. Okay. A couple more inches maybe, and I'm
24   really ready.
25   Somebody told me about some Chinese emperors
26   way back. They let their nails grow really long to show
27   they never had to work, or something. But, hey, I'm
28   working every day. Oh, yeah. I got a new job. No
29   problem. *(She laughs.)* There's this guy comes in where I
30   work. He sits around, watching me. So this one day he's
31   sitting and watching and he goes 'What're y'trying for?
32   Disability? Y' wanna be disabled? Sit home an' collect?'
33   I take a deep breath. I smile. He's a customer, after
34   all. 'It's only the one hand,' I tell him nicely, like I don't
35   give a care. So this character goes, 'It's a hand. Not a ...

1 ornament!' He shakes his head, sort of sad. 'So what's
2 it all about?' he goes. 'What goes on upstairs?' Well. I
3 feel like giving him a good slap in the face or something.
4 But then I figure he's not worth it. Here I'm maybe ready
5 for the book and I had my picture in the paper ...
6   I think like this. What's Madonna got? Nerve. And
7 Julia? That big smile. And me? I've got my nails. *(She*
8 *holds up her hand, admiring, and slowly, very slowly exits.)*
9
10
11
12
13
14
15
16
17
18
19
20
21
22
23
24
25
26
27
28
29
30
31
32
33
34
35

Trophies
by John J. Wooten

1 David — adult   Male

2

3 *(The troubled Stone family is shattered by a freak accident*

4 *that leaves the youngest son crippled and disillusioned.*

5 *David Stone, the elder son, expresses his own inner turmoil*

6 *in this candid conversation with his father. The traditional*

7 *holiday argument that follows reveals David's troublesome*

8 *thoughts and mirrors his sense of frustration with the*

9 *childish games he and his father continue to play.)*

10

11 I was up there getting my stuff together and as I packed

12 everything in my suitcase, ready to storm out of here

13 and never come back, it occurred to me what Bobby and

14 Laura said. How it gets worse for them when I come

15 home. How I use them to get at you. And I sat down and

16 looked around the room I grew up in. I tried to remember

17 what it was like being a little kid. I tried to shut my eyes

18 and force time to reverse, to take a different path. I

19 mean, that's what we both want, isn't it? Time to rewind

20 itself? Anyway, I thought of how my visits home have

21 grown uglier, shorter and less frequent. I started

22 thinking maybe I've been unfair, maybe what they said

23 was true. I was tempted to unpack the suitcase, run

24 downstairs and declare I wouldn't be leaving. I was here

25 for the duration, here to save this family. *(No response)*

26 But that would be proving Laura and Bobby wrong. And

27 as much as I hate to admit it and as much as it hurts,

28 I'm afraid I can't do that. And as pathetic as that makes

29 me feel, I don't think I can stop behaving this way. *(No*

1   *response)*
2   You see, when I was sitting up there, I couldn't
3   reverse time, no, but I could see time. Feel it. Almost
4   like I was there again. I saw a man in front of a
5   television set and he was like a statue, his eyes wouldn't
6   move. And next to him I saw a little boy, very young,
7   and he was speaking to this statue, asking it questions.
8   It was clear he was the boy's hero and the longer the
9   man remained still and distant, the more frequent and
10 desperate the questions became. And this longing grew
11 to such a point that he wanted this frozen hero of his to
12 lash out, hit him, kick him, anything. Anything to let
13 him know he was there, let him know he existed. Stupid
14 kid, huh? You and I both know there's no such thing as
15 heroes. *(No response)* Anyway, I couldn't rewind time.
16 But what I saw made me realize I no longer hate you,
17 Dad. I don't hate you because I don't think I love you
18 anymore. *(David takes a deep breath. Mr. Stone remains*
19 *motionless.)*
20
21
22
23
24
25
26
27
28
29
30
31
32
33
34
35

The Innocents Crusade
by Keith Reddin

1   Bill — sixteen   Male

2

3   *(Bill, mature at the age of sixteen, and his parents are visiting*
4   *a number of colleges in a frantic search to find a good fit for*
5   *such a gifted young man. He is seen here in the awkward*
6   *position of having to "sell himself" to an admissions officer at*
7   *a prestigious Ivy League school. Bill's interview is a*
8   *thoughtful one, but there is a measure of uncertainty in his*
9   *fanciful presentation.)*

10

11   **You see I have all this talent. I can sit down in front of**
12   **a piano and look at the music and play it, play it very**
13   **well. I started lessons very young because my parents**
14   **saw I had this natural ability. I had an affinity with**
15   **music. And I suppose I could have pursued a career,**
16   **very successfully, as a concert pianist if I wanted to, but**
17   **I realized that I would have to give everything up,**
18   **everything but my music, and I wasn't prepared for that,**
19   **you know? Also, I can draw very well. You give me a**
20   **sketch pad and a piece of charcoal and I could do a**
21   **remarkable likeness of you. I am physically very active.**
22   **I tried out for several different teams at the school. I like**
23   **tennis, I play a wicked tennis game. I'm a real net man.**
24   **I have this killer instinct, and that gets me into trouble**
25   **in a doubles game, but what can you do? I was on the**
26   **school paper. I was one of the editors, and I wrote**
27   **articles, articles on politics. That's something I might go**
28   **into down the line because I have this talent for public**
29   **speaking, for conveying ideas, and journalism. I could**

1   be a journalist, because I write well. I have the knack to
2   form ideas and communicate them in terse, concise
3   language that has been called forceful. And languages.
4   I'm a natural with languages. I studied several, but I was
5   thinking of concentrating on Latin. I think Latin is very
6   underrated right now. I think it's due for a comeback,
7   don't you? I mean, these things go in cycles. For awhile
8   Spanish and Chinese were all the rage, but I think it's
9   time for the pendulum to swing back to the basics, to
10 Latin. I was thinking about becoming a classical
11 scholar, something like that. Then there's the sciences.
12 I'm pretty exceptional with abstract concepts, physics,
13 particle physics, could do that or maybe nuclear
14 physics. That's important or astro-physics. Did you read
15 that book *A Brief History of Time*, by Stephen Hawking?
16 Neither did I. I couldn't get past page fifteen. I haven't
17 met anybody who could finish it. It was incomprehensible
18 to me. Yes, the man is brilliant I'm sure, but that book,
19 it was a best seller but I don't think anybody really read
20 it, do you? Then there's history and chemistry and
21 cartography and medicine. I could go into that. I could
22 have a very rewarding career in any of those fields, but
23 here's my problem. What do I focus on? Granted, I could
24 be one of those all around multi-career type people, but
25 in order to be the best in the field, I think I should
26 narrow my energies to one field of study. But which one,
27 that's the question. Because if I choose one over
28 another, am I then depriving myself and in a way, the
29 world, am I depriving all of us some insight, some
30 discovery, some creation, something that would lie, you
31 know, dormant till I came along? This is the dilemma I
32 face.
33
34
35

Women Behind the Walls
by Claire Braz-Valentine

1	Valdetta — early twenties	Female

2

3 *(Valdetta, a fiercely independent African-American single*
4 *mother in her early twenties, is now serving time in a*
5 *California state prison. She has been imprisoned for gross*
6 *neglect of her child, a young son who was injured in an*
7 *apartment fire while the mother was on an errand at a local*
8 *store. Now the grieving Valdetta shares the tragic story of her*
9 *son's death with Rosa, another inmate.)*

10

11 It was late, around 10 PM. We had a long day and he
12 was tired. He was sound asleep. I had to go to the store
13 to get some things for breakfast. I didn't want to wake
14 him. It was just a block away and it was freezing out. I
15 threw on my coat and ran down the three flights of
16 stairs and down the street. When I got to the store I
17 grabbed some milk and cereal and fruit. And there was
18 a lady there in front of me, arguing with the clerk. I got
19 nervous. I almost put the groceries down and ran home.
20 *(Sobs.)* Oh God how I wish I had. But I waited another
21 few minutes, and paid the clerk and raced out. I was
22 halfway up the block when I remembered the candle.
23 Our building is old and some of the lights don't work. I
24 remember covering him. I remember seeing his face, his
25 beautiful face, sleeping, seeing his face in the
26 candlelight. *(Terror at memory.)* The candle. I had left the
27 candle. It suddenly was as if I was in a dream. I was
28 running but couldn't move fast enough. I reached the
29 apartment and started climbing the stairs and then I

1 smelled the smoke. The awful smell. *(Frantic.)* I
2 remember screaming his name. David. David. Over and
3 over. Knowing I shouldn't have left him alone, and the
4 stairs going on forever, then the key, the key getting
5 stuck in the rusty old lock and the smoke coming out. I
6 remember the flames on the wall, the drapes and I ran
7 to him, screaming, 'O God please save my son, my
8 baby.' *(She picks up a bar and sits on the stage sobbing*
9 *uncontrollably, the bar across her lap. Rosa goes over, strokes*
10 *her hair. Comforts her.)*
11   But I saved him. I saved my baby. And everything
12 was going to be fine. Everything was going to be alright.
13 But the Fire Department called Children's Services and
14 they took him. They took my baby. And they put me in
15 here.
16
17
18
19
20
21
22
23
24
25
26
27
28
29
30
31
32
33
34
35

This Dream
by Heidi Decker

1 Anna — middle aged   Female
2
3   *(Anna, a middle-aged woman, sits alone on a chair in a pool*
4   *of soft light. The rest of the playing space is in stark darkness.*
5   *Although a tranquil air of calmness surrounds Anna, there is*
6   *also a foreboding sense of doom and despair hovering in the*
7   *dark clouds overhead. Her dream begins as a private*
8   *confession but moves swiftly toward something more*
9   *profound and spiritual.)*
10
11   *(Impatiently, at first)* I hate this dream. I don't know why
12   I keep having it. It's so pointless, it doesn't make any
13   sense. I mean, I've tried to look for hidden meaning, and
14   there is none. None. It's just stupid. I wish I was one of
15   those people who is able to wake themselves up from a
16   dream ... I wonder how you learn that? Hm. I thought I
17   read somewhere that it had to do with yoga. Maybe I
18   should take a class. I just ... I just hate this part. I
19   mean, when you're dreaming, you're stuck. There's
20   nothing you can do. If you don't like the dream, too bad,
21   you have to just ride it out. Just wait ... to wake up. Or
22   hope that somebody else will wake you up, which almost
23   never happens when you want it to.
24   I'm really quite disappointed in my subconscious. I'm
25   sure I can do much better than this. Everyone else has
26   fascinating recurring nightmares ... but ... well just look
27   at this! I look to be at least 20 years older, in this dark
28   little ... house. There seems to be some evidence of
29   children, hence the oatmeal and crayon mix stuck to the

1 floor. I'm always just sitting in this chair, looking out
2 the window, or cooking. Or scrubbing something. Or
3 covering my face ... stupid dream. This isn't my face. My
4 face is beautiful. Flawless. There has never been a bruise
5 on my face. Walking around ... all hunched over ... afraid
6 of everything. I'm just ... in this house. Always in this
7 house.
8   Well, it doesn't matter. This dream has absolutely
9 nothing to do with me. I just have to keep reminding
10 myself of that ... and soon enough I'll wake up and can
11 let this ridiculous experience fade away in the morning
12 sun like so much Baskerville fog. *(Very matter-of-fact)* This
13 isn't my life. My life is nothing like this ... and I certainly
14 do not look like this, or behave this way, or allow anyone
15 else to ... to ... to treat me as if ... *(Begins to falter a bit)*
16 I'm so much smarter than that. I am young. I have
17 dreams, I have potential ... I have my whole life ahead of
18 me. There is so much more to me than this ... *(Pause)* ...
19 this ... stupid, ridiculous dream.
20   I ... I'm ready to wake up now. *(Pause)* I mean it.
21 *(Slaps her cheek several times, lightly)* I **WANT TO WAKE**
22 **UP NOW!** *(Pause)* **Please, God, let me wake up.** *(She sits,*
23 *gripping the armrest of the chair, her face a desperate plea, as*
24 *the light fades down.)*
25
26
27
28
29
30
31
32
33
34
35

Racism Is, Sadly, Alive and Well
by Kimberly A. McCormick

1   Young woman   Female

2

3   *(A young woman student is making a speech at her high*

4   *school commencement ceremony. She is speaking about the*

5   *issue of prejudice. Though she hasn't been a victim of racism,*

6   *she has struggled with other prejudices because she is not*

7   *attractive. She speaks earnestly and with emotion, seeking to*

8   *persuade her audience toward positive change for the future.)*

9

10   Thank you. I want to speak to you about racism. It's so hard to

11   believe that in this day and age, there is still so much prejudice

12   around. No matter who you talk to it seems as though there's

13   at least one group of people who they have problems with for

14   one reason or another.

15   Let's see, it might be the color of a person's skin, or the way

16   their eyes slant too much, or too little, or it could be the church

17   a person goes to, the God they believe in, the way a person

18   talks, how much money their family makes, where a person

19   lives, or where their ancestors came from. You name it,

20   everyone's got some kind of hang-up.

21   I've heard that Italians have bad tempers, Scots are tight

22   with their money, Jews are all rich, African-Americans are all

23   poor, and the Irish are all too loud and obnoxious. I could go on

24   and on about all the things I've heard from other people.

25   I wouldn't have any friends if I were to listen to the

26   prejudices of others. How does this happen to us? None of us

27   are born feeling this way towards others. We're taught to be this

28   way.

29   Children are so loving and will play with anyone when they're

1   toddlers. One of my earliest memories is when my mother took
2   me to Playland. I'm caucasian and there was a little African-
3   American girl there. Right away we started playing together. I
4   noticed her skin was a different color than mine, but I thought
5   it was fascinating. She had a glow about her and her hair was
6   in all these tiny little braids that were so cool.

7   It wasn't until an older boy came up to us and said, "Don't
8   you two know that black kids don't play with white kids?" that
9   I thought maybe I was doing something wrong.

10   I ran over to my mother crying. When she heard why I was
11 upset she marched me right back to the little African-American
12 child and reminded me how much fun we were having. She said
13 to keep playing together until it was time to go. She also said
14 very loudly, so the other boy and his parents could hear, "My
15 children may play with any other children who are kind and fun
16 to play with. I want you to remember that."

17   I always have remembered my mother's words. I'm just so
18 sorry that other parents don't tell their children the same thing.

19   Getting rid of racism would be so easy if all of us would
20 make the commitment to see each other for who we are and
21 not for what we look like. Can you imagine a world where people
22 get to know each other before they decide whether or not they
23 want to continue a relationship with a person? So many good
24 friendships never happen because we look at a person and
25 decide their nose is too big, or they're too fat.

26   I am so thankful I was raised to give all people a chance. If
27 you weren't taught to believe the way I do about others, please
28 think about what I've said and make some changes in your
29 attitudes, if changes are needed. I promise you, you will meet
30 some wonderfully interesting people by doing this, and you'll
31 make some lifetime friendships you may have missed out on
32 otherwise.
33
34
35

The House of Ramon Igelsia
by Jose Rivera

1 Javier — young man   Male
2
3   *(Javier Iglesia, the oldest son and only one of three children*
4   *to attend college, believes that his father, Ramon, is a failure.*
5   *Ramon, a diabetic and drunk, plans to sell the family house*
6   *and move back to Puerto Rico. The two men fight, and*
7   *Ramon leaves the house in a fit of rage. Javier goes in search*
8   *of his father, and finds him drunken and disoriented, limping*
9   *through the snow.)*
10
11 I can just leave you here. You know that? I'll just leave
12 you here and you can die in the cold. I'll leave you here
13 if I want!
14   Half of me wants to do that. Lie right down there,
15 Dad! Cover yourself up! Go to sleep! Let them find you
16 tomorrow morning. You'll be doing me a favor. I won't
17 have to point to you, saying, 'That's my father, that
18 janitor there! See the bent old man with the mop? The
19 old slave dragging his feet? That's my proud old man!'
20 *(Ramon falls in the snow)* GET UP FOR CHRISSAKES!
21 Don't you have any pride at all? Are you going to let this
22 snow kill you while I stand here watching you? If you
23 don't get up, I'll walk, I'll leave, I swear! *(Bending down*
24 *over his father)* Why can't you help yourself? Why? *(Low)*
25 Why can't you help ... yourself? You should never have
26 bent down so I could wipe my feet on your back. I never
27 asked you to do that for me. Why did you do that for
28 me? Why were you that way for me? Why did you suffer
29 so ... quietly?

A Moment's Peace
by Keith A. Scollick

1   Young woman   Female
2
3   *(A young woman has been diagnosed HIV positive and calls*
4   *her married lover late at night in the hope of finding 'a*
5   *moment's peace.' It is a dark night of trauma for the solitary*
6   *figure in search of peaceful, internal solitude to face*
7   *insurmountable odds. Trembling from fear, with a slight*
8   *touch of drowsiness, she reaches for the phone and slowly*
9   *dials a number from memory.)*
10
11 There is no need to get upset. You don't need to yell at
12 me. Yes, you are. Listen, will you please listen for a
13 moment? I've got something big to tell you. You
14 probably should sit down for this. It goes beyond what
15 you're thinking. This was just meant to ease the blow.
16 Are you sitting? ... *(Takes a deep breath)* I don't know
17 where to start. It's not like there is a true beginning.
18 Well, *(Fumbling a little)* I guess ... remember the last time
19 the bloodmobile was at work? I gave blood like I always
20 do. It's no big deal. I've tried to donate at least twice a
21 year. Anyway, a while later, I get a call asking me to
22 come in for a blood test. The doctor checked me over
23 asking me a lot of questions. I went back two more
24 times ... I didn't want you to know because I didn't want
25 you to worry ... Well, I'm telling you now. Anyway, she
26 checked me over, and I knew there was something she
27 wasn't telling me, but I never suspected ...
28   I got a call this evening ... I'm HIV positive. *(She*
29 *sighs, collects her thoughts and continues on almost without*

1   *breath.)* **The** nurse told me just like that. No preparation,
2   no ready, set, go. She told me flatly just like that, as if
3   I was like the thirtieth person she had to tell that day.
4   *(More to herself)* **God** help me if I was ... She went on to
5   tell me that it wasn't AIDS, yet, and I should learn and
6   understand the distinction as if it really matters. 'You
7   can still lead a productive and full life.' It's just that you
8   are carrying something for which there is no cure now or
9   in the foreseeable future. It may not get you today, or
10   tomorrow, or maybe even ten years from now, but it will
11   get you. Once you have it, it won't go away. 'Have a
12   pleasant rest of your life.'
13   At first I didn't cry. I didn't know what to do. It
14   happened so fast, it's almost as if I wasn't hearing it. I felt
15   removed, detached from it all as ... as if watching myself
16   not really interacting. I can see my reaction as plain as
17   day. The initial shock turning to horror and *(Starts to cry)* ...
18   I can't do this alone. I don't want to go through this alone
19   *(Long pause)* ... Please say something ... How? ... That's
20   all you can say is how? Is it that important to you? The
21   need to brand me, put me into some neat little group so
22   people can marvel at me and watch me like some circus
23   side-show freak. You know I don't do drugs, and I'm not a
24   hemophiliac. So, what you want to know is if I've been
25   sleeping around. Is that why you won't answer me?
26   *(Shouting)* I WANT TO KNOW IF YOU LOVE ME. I want to
27   know what's going through your mind. Are you hurt? Are
28   you trapped? Are you relieved to know that it's out in the
29   open? Well, I can tell you that you're the only person I've
30   slept with in the past year, and I know I didn't have this
31   damn virus before I met you.
32   It was hard for me to accept that I was sharing your
33   life with your wife, but that's more my fault. But, how
34   many others are there? How many more have you made
35   feel like they were something special and cared for them

1   only so that you could ... toss them aside? I love you. I
2   care and desire you as I have no one else I've ever met.
3   And, to show for it all I get for my vulnerability is
4   betrayal and a disease. Excuse me, 'syndrome.' Wham,
5   bang. It was good, now it's deadly. It's only the first
6   night I've known, but I can feel it in me. The blood
7   pumping through my heart carrying it, infecting every
8   part of my body. Nowhere is safe, my toes, my fingers,
9   my heart ... not even my brain. Every thought conceived
10   from now on tainted and tarnished because it was
11   supplied by it. No more looking at myself in the mirror.
12   I don't see myself anymore. I just see it pumping
13   through me, destroying me. You're not supposed to be
14   able to see it, but I do. I know it's there, and that's
15   enough.
16
17
18
19
20
21
22
23
24
25
26
27
28
29
30
31
32
33
34
35

Wasp

by Steve Martin

1 Kathryn (Sis) — young girl   Female

2

3   *(The delightful, wacky comedian Steve Martin offers a*

4   *whimsical, bittersweet "spoof" on traditional family life that*

5   *features zany family portraits. Sis (Kathryn), a young girl*

6   *facing an unimaginable adult future, celebrates Christmas*

7   *with a comic spirit that bears the unmistakable imprint of*

8   *satire. Here, Sis manages to reduce every serious holiday*

9   *tradition to absurdity 'On Christmas Day.')*

10

11   **On Christmas Day ...**

12   **I guess pretty pink ears don't count for much. How can**

13   **I possibly pay attention? How can I possibly focus on**

14   **this little tune when I am so much more fascinating?**

15   **Those who pass within the area of my magnetism know**

16   **what I'm talking about. My power extends not just to**

17   **the length of my arms but all around me when I pass in**

18   **the hallways, lockers, to those who hear my voice. I am**

19   **a flame and I bring myself to the unsuspecting moths.**

20   **Unnaturally and strangely the power ceases when I'm**

21   **home. There, my sphere of influence stays within here**

22   **(She indicates her head), all within. It's all silent in the**

23   **presence of my mother and father and brother. What**

24   **they don't realize is that one idea from this little mind**

25   **changes the course of rivers. Not to mention families.**

26   **Sorry. (Pause) I know from where my salvation will**

27   **come. I will give birth to the baby Jesus. The baby**

28   **Jesus brought to you by Kathryn, the near virgin. I will**

29   **have to buy swaddling clothes. The sweet baby Jesus,**

1   the magician. He will wave his hand and the dishes will

2   wash themselves and he will wave his other hand and

3   the water on the dishes will bead up and rise to the

4   heavens in a reverse dish-drying rain. I will put them

5   away. And I will sweetly cradle him. People will come to

6   him for miracles and I will look proudly on. He will grow

7   and become my husband, the true virgin and the near-

8   virgin. Both of us perfectly unspoiled, perfectly true. He

9   couldn't work the miracles without me. I would run the

10   mini-mart and be the inspiration, the wife of Jesus. And

11   at the end of our lives, he would become the baby Jesus

12   again and I would put him in the swaddling clothes and

13   carry him upward, entering heaven in a beaded dress

14   that weighed so much she could hardly stand up

15   straight. But she did, this tiny girl from the Southland,

16   her pupils made small from the flashbulbs. *(Sings)*

17   On Christmas Day.

18   On Christmas Day.

19   I saw three ships a sailing

20   On Christmas Day in the morning.

21

22

23

24

25

26

27

28

29

30

31

32

33

34

35

Silent No More
by Gus Edwards

1   Harris — late twenties   Male
2
3   *(Harris, an African-American male in his late twenties,*
4   *defends himself — and other African-American males —*
5   *against suspicious, cold and uncaring "black sisters." There*
6   *is a sense of urgency voiced in his need to address distrustful*
7   *and suspicious sisters. But it is in the fierce internal struggle*
8   *taking place that Harris catches a fleeting glance of his own*
9   *spirit and soul.)*
10
11   I agreed to going on that TV talk show because I think
12   it's about time one of us talked back. Black brothers, I
13   mean. Man, if you listen to all the stuff you hear about
14   us on them shows and believe what they write about us
15   in magazines, then you got to think that the black man
16   is maybe the worst species of human being God ever
17   created. Because besides all the criminal things they tell
18   you we done and continue to do, they also tell you that
19   we lazy, low-minded, drunk or drugged up most of the
20   time, and that we don't know how to treat our women.
21   More than we don't know how to treat them, we don't
22   even know how to see any beauty in them. You see we
23   all walking around blind except when some white woman
24   pass our way, I guess. I don't know. But that's what
25   they put in the magazines. And on TV. And I'm not just
26   talking about white people either. I'm talking about our
27   black sisters. Some of them anyway. They the ones you
28   see on them talk shows talking about what bad role
29   models we are. And what a shame that is. And one that

1   I was watching the other day, she jumped up in front of
2   the camera and said: 'Let's talk it plain, black men are
3   dogs!' Man, the whole audience just clap their hands
4   and shout back to her, 'That's right, Sister! You telling
5   the truth. They is dogs, every one of them!' ... And I sat
6   there thinking, I ain't no dog. And I don't appreciate
7   nobody calling me one. Especially on TV. If somebody
8   had say that to my face I would knock them down. I
9   don't care how big they are, or how small.
10   I grew up respecting women and I expect them to
11   respect me, too. My mother was a woman and I
12   respected her. When I got to a certain age, she
13   respected me, too. That's the way I think things should
14   be. 'Do unto others as you would have them do unto
15   you' is the rule I grew up with. And I try to live by it. But
16   it don't seem like too many people go by that any more.
17   Especially when they get on TV. It's like that camera
18   give them a license to curse you, insult you, and call you
19   any bad name they wish. And you, 'cause you're a man,
20   ain't supposed to say nothing about it. You supposed to
21   take it quietly and keep your mouth shut. I mean, those
22   people assassinating your character to a million people
23   and you ain't supposed to say a damn thing except to
24   agree. And maybe stand up in front of everybody like
25   they do at AA meetings and say, 'My name is So-and-
26   So. I am a black man; therefore, I am a dog.' I don't
27   think so. And I ain't doing it. Hell, no. In fact I'm doing
28   just the opposite. I'm going on that TV show and let the
29   world hear my side of things. And when I do, I ain't gon'
30   be speaking for every black man. I'm going to be
31   speaking just for me. The rest of them don't want to
32   talk, that's their business. I know for me, I just don't
33   want to be silent no more.
34
35

All My Tomorrows
by Rick Doble

1   Unnamed — elderly   Female
2
3   *(An unnamed elderly character is devoted to watching*
4   *Chester Maddox on the television soap opera* All My
5   Tomorrows. *Here is an intimate glimpse of the daily life of a*
6   *soap opera addict. There is a basic human frailty revealed in*
7   *the character's simple confessions, but there is also a blend of*
8   *sadness reflected in the dull and ordinary life that offers no*
9   *alternative to the handsome Chester Maddox.)*
10
11   Chester Maddox, you devil! I rode for two hours in the
12   snow to see you. An old friend from Carson Mills gave
13   me a ride. You know, I wrote weeks ago I'd be there this
14   weekend. But you didn't show. I've really had it with
15   you, I have. For twenty years I've spent each afternoon
16   following your devious ways. Like the time you tricked
17   Cynthia into marriage, then abandoned her, after she
18   lost her memory, in some town out west. Now, I'm not
19   forgetting you tried to redeem yourself. You did rescue
20   the young girl from that mob of terrorists, but only
21   because Jessie asked. We all knew, of course, that
22   Jessica was your one true love. Oh yes, I can see
23   through you. Handsome and dashing, able to charm
24   them all, even those who don't want to trust you. But
25   this time I'm finished. I've written you for years, let you
26   know every detail of my life. And even though you never
27   answered, I felt a bond had grown between us. So when
28   I read you'd be this close, that the entire cast of *All My*
29   *Tomorrows* would be in Providence, I made sure I'd meet

1   you. I waited an hour in the freezing cold. Chester

2   Maddox what am I going to do about you?

3   I'm here at my window watching my ducks across

4   the water near the point. Tears of anger are filling my

5   eyes at what you've done to me. But I'm not the first.

6   Suppose I won't be the last. I'm lying on the couch in

7   my 'jelly' house. It used to sit on the highway where

8   they sold jams and such to the tourists before it was

9   moved. In spite of today I feel so lucky. I have this cozy

10   little place I can afford, because, you know, there are all

11   those expensive mansions across the way. And I've got

12   my cats and my beloved ducks on my pond. I retired

13   here. I'm sure I wrote you about it, from the mill where

14   I'd worked my way, over the years, to floor manager,

15   2nd shift. My friends were certain I'd be lonely, away

16   from the clacking looms. But you know, Chester, I really

17   don't miss it.

18   I feed the wild mallards and know each of their

19   ducklings by sight. My cats with bells around their

20   throats run free in the graveyard. I watch the seasons

21   change through my picture window, from white to brown

22   to green and back. The sun glances through the plate

23   glass differently each month. In winter the TV's good, in

24   summer it's all reruns. Except yours, Chester. Each

25   afternoon I see your life progressing with mine, as we

26   grow old together. You've lasted so long you're almost

27   treated with respect, achieved a certain status by

28   surviving. Odd for such a scoundrel as you. Oh dear, it's

29   getting dark.

30   Where are my cats? I guess I'm going to have to call

31   them, stand on the porch, bang my spoon and sauce

32   pan. They're such devils staying out so late. And after I

33   finally coax them home, I'll feed them and brush their

34   fur. Then I'll open a can of soup, and settle back onto

35   this couch to watch those sitcoms I don't like nearly as

much as my soaps. But that's life and I have to accept it. In the evening that's about all there is. And on Monday we'll see about you, Mr. Maddox. When two o'clock rolls around, I might not watch *All My Tomorrows*, just to get even. Except knowing you, I won't be able to resist. So I probably will.

Two
by Jim Cartwright

1   Mrs. Iger — fifties   Female

2

3   *(Mrs. Iger, an aging but jolly woman in her fifties, sits on a*
4   *bar stool in an English pub with arms folded and head*
5   *slightly cocked. Glancing around, she shares her notion of*
6   *the "ideal man" with all who will listen. Like an archeologist*
7   *unearthing a lost species, Mrs. Iger delights in the dreams of*
8   *robust Roman centurions, rock-solid and god-like, to help*
9   *rekindle her vivid imagination.)*

10

11   I love big men. Big quiet strong men. That's all I want.
12   I love to tend to them. I like to have grace and flurry
13   round them. I like their temple arms and pillar legs and
14   synagogue chests and big mouth and teeth and tongue
15   like an elephant's ear. And big carved faces like a
16   natural cliff side, and the Roman empire bone work. And
17   you can really dig deep into 'em, can't you? And there's
18   so much. Gargantuan men, like a Roman Empire, with
19   a voice he hardly uses, but when he does it's all
20   rumbling under his breast plate. So big, big hands, big
21   everything. Like sleeping by a mountain side. Carved
22   men. It's a thrill if you see them run, say for a bus,
23   pounding up the pavement. Good big man, thick blood
24   through tubular veins, squirting and washing him out. It
25   must be like a bloody red cavernous car wash in there,
26   in him, and all his organs and bits hanging from the rib
27   roof, getting a good daily drenching in this good red
28   blood. They are so bloody big you think they'll never die,
29   and that's another reason you want them. Bloody ox

1 men. Hercules, Thor, Chuck Connors, come on, bring
2 your heads down and take from my 'ickle hand. Let me
3 groom and coddle you. And herd you. Yes, let me gather
4 all you big men of our Isles and herd you up and lead you
5 across America. You myth men. Myth men. Myth men.
6 Big men, love ya!
7
8
9
10
11
12
13
14
15
16
17
18
19
20
21
22
23
24
25
26
27
28
29
30
31
32
33
34
35

Feeding the Pelicans
by Ryan Leone

1   Unspecified   Male/Female

2

3   *(The challenge in playing non-dramatic audition material —*

4   *literature adapted or edited from sources other than theatre*

5   *scripts — is to make daring choices. The following poem, for*

6   *example, presents a dramatic figure you might consider for an*

7   *audition performance. See if you can design a character*

8   *portrait that captures the age, vocal range, and movement*

9   *potential for the poetic character suggested.)*

10

11   What is it at the end of the pier, where

12   the mud-caked pelicans dive in arcs

13   like bending rays of sunlight

14   that makes me long

15   for their life?

16   Is it how they lose themselves

17   in the breath of each second

18   as their bodies glide

19   over the black water, flying in between

20   the lights of the rippling stars?

21

22   Is it the single bird, carving

23   his hunger like marble

24   into the sky, until it drops suddenly,

25   riding an inch over the water

26   with a silverfish broken into its bill?

27

28   Either way,

29   I drag them into my life

1   to remind me of the possibility
2   of being that stirs
3   in my bones like a dream.
4
5   How the wind loosens itself
6   into my body
7   as if I were a ghost,
8   a cloud being bullied around.
9   How the wind renders this offering of grief
10   as no more than a gesture,
11   a cry in the vacuum
12   of the natural world.
13
14
15
16
17
18
19
20
21
22
23
24
25
26
27
28
29
30
31
32
33
34
35

Doppelganger
by Jo. J. Adamson

1	A model — unspecified	Female

3   *(An attractive model strikes candid poses for a willing*
4   *photographer on the deck of a cruise ship. In an elaborate*
5   *ritual of artificial posing and polite conversation, the model*
6   *offers a candid view of the false glitter that surrounds her life.*
7   *Look at the title of the script for a faint hint of a sinister*
8   *undercurrent at work here. Doppelganger: a ghostly*
9   *counterpart of a living person.)*

11   **A thousand things go through my head as the**
12   **photographer checks the light. Is my lipstick glossy?**
13   **Cheeks luminous? Figure voluptuous? Eyes bright, teeth**
14   **pearly? Hair curly? Will I project the right image?** *(Trying*
15   *different poses)* **Vacationing? Young Miss Contemplating?**
16   **Ingenue Visits Atlanta. Society Deb. On Verandah.**
17   **Young Beauty Soaks up Sun. American Miss Visits**
18   **Venice. Austrian Lass Studies Sunset. Fraulein Heinler**
19   **Smiles at Photographer. Mademoiselle Cline Boards**
20   **Luxury Liner.** *(Photographer adjusts his equipment while*
21   *she powders her nose.)* **Focus your lens on my tight skin.**
22   **I was born for the close-up. The sun is my friend. I open**
23   **like a flower. Come to me. Come on. Photograph the**
24   **light around my cells. The shadow of my smile. Soft**
25   **focus me on to the edge of eternity. I'm the infinite**
26   **closing of your iris shot. The particle in your eye that**
27   **won't wash out. Feel me to the whorls of your fingers.**
28   **Preserve the dream emulsion in your soul. Embalm the**
29   **celluloid daylights out of me and I'll look good in**

1   tomorrow's photogravure. *(Trying different poses again)*
2   How do you want me? It's a rhetorical question.
3   Fetching? Perhaps. Whimsical, capricious, coquettish, to
4   be sure. Here's Pert, Saucy, Bewitching ... Alluring. I
5   give you Tantalizing, Teasing, Tempting, always. Toss of
6   head, angle of chin, curve of neck always right up to the
7   orgasmic dissolve.
8   *(Addressing the photographer)* We work well together.
9   Where do you stop and I begin? I await your separation
10   in safe-light suspension. OK, I'm ready. Click the
11   shutter. *(She becomes flustered, unsure.)* I'm all aflutter.
12   You'd think I'd be used to this. Each time is like the first
13   virgin thrust. One more minute, my make-up's running,
14   nose shiny ... No! I'm beauty's perfection. The stuff
15   dreams are made of. 'No sweat' as they say. Click the
16   shutter while the feeling rises. Take the wave at its crest.
17   Now! Fire when ready, sir. I'm at my best!
18
19
20
21
22
23
24
25
26
27
28
29
30
31
32
33
34
35

The Big Funk
by John Patrick Shanley

1   Austin — twenties   Male

2

3   *(Austin, an actor and young man in his twenties, faces an*
4   *uneasy East Village, New York City audience. Austin,*
5   *speaking impromptu, expresses his views on human nature*
6   *and politics. He is both spirited and theatrical in his*
7   *presentation. Following a series of comic turns and half-stated*
8   *notions, Austin issues a patriotic call for the audience to rise*
9   *up and seek a more meaningful reality.)*

10

11   **Hi. My name's Austin. I believe in live and let live. I**
12   **swear to God nobody believes in this but me. I'm in my**
13   **house. I'm doin' what I do when I'm not doin' what I do.**
14   **I'm an actor. And people come around, call, people try**
15   **to get me to go here, do this, believe that, eat this,**
16   **change my hair, change my clothes, my manners, my**
17   **posture. I'll tell you this: It don't make me feel loved.**
18   **And this is a battle. 'Cause people wanna tell you what**
19   **to do. And they're looking for an angle, any angle, a way**
20   **in. If they find out maybe you're a little shaky about your**
21   **nose, then they'll talk about your nose all the time.**
22   **How's your nose today? How do you feel about your**
23   **nose? You must be upset about your nose. What are you**
24   **gonna do about your nose? Until you scream in their**
25   **face and tell 'em to get outta your business. Or you get**
26   **a nose job. And if you do that, then they got you. This**
27   **one part a you's not you anymore. It's somebody else's**
28   **idea of how you should be. You're on your way to**
29   **becoming somebody you don't know. A doll in dress-up**

1   clothes. But what? No. I don't. But sometimes I feel like
2   it's me or them, me or society. I believe in live and let
3   live, but society don't. You think we live in a time where
4   everybody does what they want? You are wrong! You
5   should talk to me. Somebody should be talking to me.
6   'Cause in me and people like me I do believe lies a better
7   world.
8   We don't know how to make it better anymore than
9   anybody else. But I'll tell you the main thing about me
10   that makes what I just said so. I am a constructive
11   person. *(Goes down into the audience.)* A constructive
12   person. What's that? Maybe it's a hero waitin' to happen.
13   But there are no job listings in the paper under hero.
14   Heroes often go their whole lives unemployed. And in a
15   way, that's what I hope happens. Because what if I'm
16   wrong and I'm not a hero? I've never been tested. If I'm
17   not tested, my tombstone should be carved into the
18   shape of a big question mark. We could do something. I
19   don't wanna settle. We could make things a lot better
20   than they are. I know! You can explain why I'm wrong.
21   Why the streets have to be dirty and the politicians have
22   to be corrupt and drugs and starvation, and why there's
23   cruelty right there in your face and you can't do anything
24   about it. But you're wrong! Listen to me! I'm not wrong!
25   We could make things better than they are. Living your
26   life is supposed to make you weary. That's what death is
27   for. Rest! You can't be lazy. You need to call up your
28   guts. 'Cause it's just cowardice to say, 'Oh, that's the
29   way things are. You can't do nothing about that.' I'm
30   telling you, Brothers and Sisters, we could be heroes!
31
32
33
34
35

Big Ball: The Family Play
by Leslie Bramm

1   Billy — eighteen   Male
2
3   *(Billy, an eighteen-year-old young man, is hopelessly adrift*
4   *with no apparent meaning or purpose in life. He is a lonely*
5   *figure entangled in a troubled family web, struggling to*
6   *regain a sense of personal identity. Here, he recalls a family*
7   *fishing trip and an incident with a small pack of whales that*
8   *gave meaning and purpose to his understanding of the*
9   *mysterious truth of life.)*
10
11   He said they would start bumping the boat next if we
12   didn't leave and his old rig couldn't take it. 'So what?
13   Who cares? Sink it. Sink it all!' We're motoring away,
14   and the bull is getting smaller, and I'm stuck. I'm gonna
15   be stuck here. Stuck right here forever! DOESN'T
16   ANYBODY GET IT!
17   The next thing I know, I'm in the water. I don't even
18   remember jumping in. I take off after the whales. I swim
19   and swim. I swim until my arms ache and my legs are
20   like rubber. My heart is pounding out of my chest, but I
21   can breathe. I can breathe better. I can breathe easier.
22   I'm there. I'm with them. We're rolling and diving and
23   laughing ... I see the boat. A little dot on the horizon ...
24   Then it's gone ... The remnants of gas and oil are all
25   that's left. No trace of them at all. Just the blue, blue
26   ocean ... I dive under. I can hold my breath just like
27   them, and I see crusty stuff clinging to my ribs. My feet
28   ... They're flat and blue and I don't have any toes, and
29   this thing, I can feel it, between my shoulder blades. It

1   puckers, then opens wide. I arch my back and let it
2   break the surface. I can breathe ... I gulp in a massive
3   rush of air ... One thrust of my mighty tail and I'm off
4   with this pack, this pod, this family of mine ... I could
5   hate them. My family. I could hear their voices, in my
6   head, the rest of my life. I could nurture this perfectly,
7   perfect hate. I could hate blind, hate cold, hate pure. I
8   could learn to hate really well, become a master-hater.
9   Hate the world, hate myself. I could let that hate of Hugh
10   and Madge drown everything else ... Or I could do what
11   any good whale does and swim away ... Just swim away.
12   Just swim away.
13
14
15
16
17
18
19
20
21
22
23
24
25
26
27
28
29
30
31
32
33
34
35

Under Siege
by G. L. Horton

1   Maria — adult   Female
2
3   *(Maria, a young woman with four children, is a battered and*
4   *pregnant wife now going through counseling before a*
5   *scheduled abortion. The setting is a family clinic, and Maria*
6   *speaks to her counselor in short, crisp lines of dialog. The*
7   *atmosphere is abruptly charged with tension as Maria begins*
8   *to imagine the senseless violence that may surface if her*
9   *husband discovers she is pregnant with her boyfriend's child.)*
10
11   If I started to show, and he found out, my husband
12   would use it in court to take the children. He doesn't
13   want children. All he does is yell and hit us. But I guess
14   he wants to make us suffer because he can't always be
15   the king of everything any more. So he's fighting me for
16   the custody. I feel terrible, to have an abortion, to kill my
17   innocent baby. But it's life against life. If my husband
18   found out he would kill all of us! He would find my
19   boyfriend and smash him to pieces! He is a monster.
20   You see this? He did this to me. And others, many
21   others. That's why I have to divorce him. My family
22   says, he's your husband. A husband is for life. If he
23   beats you, you must change and do what he says, so he
24   will be good to you. But I say, this husband is for death.
25   And I am going to get away from him and be happy. No,
26   my family mustn't know. They might tell him! I can't
27   even tell my sister. She would want to help me. She
28   would try, but she has a big mouth and I can't be sure
29   it won't get back to him. My boyfriend. He will help me.

1   I won't have to tell him why, he will help. Whatever I do.
2   This is a wonderful man whose baby I'm carrying, a
3   gentle man. He treats me like a queen. *(Begins to cry)* I'm
4   sorry. I want to have this baby. I didn't mean to cry. I
5   thought my crying was all over. I'm so sorry. It makes
6   me feel so bad. I thought I was going to be all right. I
7   thought I'd finally gotten away from him, and here one
8   more time he's running my life. Like a wicked king.
9   Ruining my life.
10
11
12
13
14
15
16
17
18
19
20
21
22
23
24
25
26
27
28
29
30
31
32
33
34
35

Class Action
by Brad Slaight

1   Emma — teen   Female

2

3   *(Emma, a naive high school student, recounts a traumatic*
4   *encounter at a recent rock concert. There is a quiet intensity*
5   *at the beginning of her conversation that culminates in a*
6   *chilling confession. Emma's frightening experience is a*
7   *bittersweet, coming-of-age realization of emotional turmoil*
8   *and mental anguish as she struggles to deal with her own*
9   *sense of isolation and vulnerability.)*

10

11   I screamed when the DJ told me I had not only won
12   tickets to the concert, but backstage passes as well.
13   *(She displays a backstage pass.)* I mean I had never won
14   anything in my life, and then all of a sudden I was caller
15   number twenty-five and on my way to the biggest
16   concert of the year! The New Landlords were my favorite
17   group, and the fact that I was going to get to meet them
18   kept me from getting much sleep the rest of the week.
19   The concert was everything I hoped it would be. I had
20   the best seat in the house and my friend Cindy owed me
21   big time for giving her the other ticket. She just about
22   passed out when we went backstage to meet the band
23   members. Eddie was my favorite and I almost fainted
24   when they introduced him to me. He was the lead
25   singer, and not really that much older than me, even
26   though he looked like he was. Cindy was so caught up
27   with all the excitement, she didn't see Eddie and me
28   leave the party and go to his dressing room. *(Pause.)*
29   I guess I should have known what was going on, but

1   I honestly thought we were just going to get away from
2   the noise and have a good talk. Eddie and me alone
3   together, it was like a dream or something! His lyrics are
4   so inspiring, so full of love that I was completely shocked
5   when he pulled me over to a couch and started tearing
6   at my clothes. Maybe if he would have kissed me or
7   something first I wouldn't have reacted like I did, but he
8   moved on me so quick. He got on top of me and started
9   pulling at my shirt. He was much stronger than me and
10   even though I pushed and told him no, he pinned me
11   down. I started to panic because I felt trapped and he
12   wouldn't listen to me. His rough beard was scratching
13   my face. His breath made me nauseous. When he
14   started to unzip his pants it gave me just enough room
15   to swing my knee hard into his crotch, causing him to
16   fall off me. I got out of there before he could go any
17   further. *(Pause.)* I saw him on MTV the next week. He had
18   makeup on, but I could still see the scratch marks where
19   I gouged his face. I hope it never heals. *(She looks at the*
20   *backstage pass and tosses it on the ground as she exits.)*
21
22
23
24
25
26
27
28
29
30
31
32
33
34
35

The Path
by Erica Lustig

1   Unspecified   Male/Female
2
3   *(A brooding, lonely character speaks in a hushed voice to a*
4   *non-existent friend and pleads for compassion and*
5   *understanding. The disillusioned character is driven by a fear*
6   *of inadequacy and consumed with self-doubt. There is aching*
7   *sorrow in the constant struggle to try to make sense of life's*
8   *misfortune and the desire to act out life with a sense of passion*
9   *and purpose.)*
10
11   I'm so confused right now, and each thing I do and say
12   just confuses me even more to the point of fear. How far
13   can the confusion go until I can't even control the course
14   of my own life anymore? I'm confused about everything:
15   love, friendship, faith, religion, goals, beauty, memories,
16   pain, life, death, everything. Mostly love, for it really IS
17   all of those things listed. I've tried reaching deep inside
18   myself to better understand all these things, to find the
19   answers to all my questions for I'm told and tell myself
20   they're deep within me. I come up empty. There's no
21   one to turn to. I just get different mixed answers that
22   confuse me more so, therefore, I am trapped. Lonely. I
23   do not know where this blank spot in life will take me
24   nor do I yearn to find out. But I'm being blindly led down
25   a path that I'm not sure I want to go down and I'm
26   kicking and screaming all the way. Each step makes a
27   certain part of my life confusing!
28   What I most fear is getting to the end of the path
29   and finding the inevitable truths and answers to my

1 questions that I ache so badly to know, yet fear what
2 they may be. So now what? Can anybody help me? Hear
3 my pleas? Is anyone out there? Or is this just another
4 one of those things I must do myself ... I can't. Yet they
5 say can't is not a real word, there is no 'can't.' There's
6 one thing I've found, there IS a can't. I CAN'T find love
7 and I CAN'T find peace and I just CAN'T seem to be
8 able to do anything that I want to. So what does that
9 mean? If my life is full of can'ts then does that mean I'm
10 headed towards some kind of doom? Is that where this
11 twisted path is headed? Then HELP ME! SOMEONE! I
12 CAN'T do this alone. Or can I? I am so weak, so small,
13 so young and confused and I will always be this way. I
14 guess that's what's meant to be.
15   Is it? Do you know? Do I? No. I don't know anything.
16 It's all up to you now. It's all up to you, brain,
17 conscience, heart. It's all up to you, friend. Nonexistent
18 friend, there are no friends. No one, no one but me and
19 I am frail and weak, headed nowhere. Blind on the path,
20 no one to lead me. Please lead me ... please.
21
22
23
24
25
26
27
28
29
30
31
32
33
34
35

Boys' Life
by Howard Korder

1 Phil — adult   Male
2
3 *(Phil, an anxious underachiever with low self-esteem, meets*
4 *regularly with college chums to complain about his lack of*
5 *success in finding the right girl. His sexual sob stories,*
6 *usually revolving around the most recent romantic tragedy,*
7 *are legendary and laughable to his friends. In this latest*
8 *installment, Phil describes the brief fling he recently had with*
9 *an equally neurotic Karen.)*
10
11 I would have destroyed myself for this woman. Gladly. I
12 would have eaten garbage. I would have sliced my wrists
13 open. Under the right circumstances, I mean, if she
14 said, 'Hey, Phil, why don't you just cut your wrists
15 open?' Well, come on, but if seriously ... We clicked, we
16 connected on so many things, right off the bat, we
17 talked about God for three hours once. I don't know
18 what good it did, but that intensity ... and the first time
19 we went to bed, I didn't even touch her. I didn't want to,
20 understand what I'm saying? And you know, I played it
21 very casually, because, all right, I've had some rough
22 experiences, I'm the first to admit, but after a couple of
23 weeks I could feel we were right there, so I laid it down,
24 everything I wanted to tell her, and ... and she says to
25 me ... She says ... 'Nobody should ever need another
26 person that badly.' Do you believe that? 'Nobody should
27 ever ... !' What is that? Is that something you saw on
28 TV? I dump my heart on the table, you give me Dr.
29 Joyce Brothers? 'Need, need,' I'm saying I love you, is

1   that wrong? Is that not allowed anymore? *(Pause. Jack*
2   *looks at him.)* **And so what if I did need her? Is that so**
3   **bad? All right, crucify me, I needed her!**
4   So what! I don't want to be my myself. I'm by myself
5   I feel like I'm going out of my mind, I do. I sit there, I'm
6   thinking forget it, I'm not gonna make it through the next
7   ten seconds. I just can't stand it. But I do, somehow, I
8   get through the ten seconds, but then I have to do it all
9   over again, 'cause they just keep coming, all these ...
10   seconds, floating by, while I'm waiting for something to
11   happen, I don't know what, a car wreck, a nuclear war or
12   something, that sounds awful but at least there'd be this
13   instant when I'd know I was alive. Just once. 'Cause I
14   look in the mirror, and I can't believe I'm really there. I
15   can't believe that's me. It's like my body, right, is the
16   size of, what, the Statue of Liberty, and I'm inside it, I'm
17   down in one of the legs, this gigantic hairy leg, I'm
18   scraping around inside my own foot like some tiny fetus.
19   And I don't know who I am or where I'm going. And I
20   wish I'd never been born. *(Pause)* **Not only that, my hair**
21   **is falling out, and that really sucks.** *(Pause)*
22
23
24
25
26
27
28
29
30
31
32
33
34
35

Rememberin' Stuff
by Eleanor Harder

1   Maxine — young adult   Female

2

3   *(Maxine, a young unwed mother, is in group therapy*

4   *learning to cope with the harsh reality of having to raise a*

5   *small child alone. She is a vulnerable single parent who*

6   *appears even more fragile when she begins to unearth*

7   *intimate memories to share with the group. "Rememberin'*

8   *stuff" encourages the sensitive Maxine to understand she has*

9   *a good helping of strength and the will to survive.)*

10

11   **Well, let's see.** *(To GROUP and audience.)* **Well, uh ... I**

12   **remember that from the time I was real little, I always**

13   **wanted a baby of my own. And when I was sixteen I got**

14   **pregnant, and — now I've got one.** *(Short uncomfortable*

15   *pause, then she continues.)* **And I remembered thinkin'**

16   **that if I had a baby, I'd always have somebody to love**

17   **and somebody who'd love me. Because nobody else**

18   **had. Not really, y'know? And then, I — I thought**

19   **everybody would look up to me, think I was special,**

20   **because I had a kid.** *(Sighs.)* **Well, I have a kid now, and**

21   **yeah, I love him and all, and I guess he loves me. But, I**

22   **don't know, it sure isn't the way I thought it was gonna**

23   **be. I mean, like the cute cuddly little puppy I had once?**

24   **Not. Man, I didn't know a baby was so much work. And**

25   **I worry when he grows up he might not love me**

26   **anymore, y'know? I mean, some kids don't.** *(Shakes*

27   *head.)*

28   **There's so much stuff to worry about! Like, when**

29   **he's sick and screams all night, and his daddy — hmph!**

1   He never comes around or helps or anything. Don't even
2   know where he is now. And I don't know how I'm gonna
3   manage alone. But, hey. *(Motions toward BABY.)* It's not
4   his fault. He's just a little baby. And I do love him. I
5   really do. It's just — well, I remember thinkin' that
6   havin' a kid would make everything all right, y'know?
7   Change everything. Well, it sure changed everything all
8   right. Y'know? Change everything. Well, it sure changed
9   everything, but it didn't make everything all right. But
10   *(Shrugs)* you know, maybe nothin' ever does. Make
11   things right, I mean. *(BABY cries. To BABY.)* All right, all
12   right, I'm comin.' *(Goes to carseat and picks up BABY, then*
13   *turns to GROUP.)* Hey, I gotta go. See you guys around —
14   *(Shrugs)* sometime. Huh?
15
16
17
18
19
20
21
22
23
24
25
26
27
28
29
30
31
32
33
34
35

Man and God: Having a Few Beers and Talking Things Over
by Jeffrey Scott

1   The following script features multiple voices and is
2   appropriate for partner auditions or the rehearsal period.
3   This brief, but complete, script is typical of those absurd
4   comedies that call attention to solitary figures struggling to
5   gain an understanding of the mysterious truth of life. The
6   simple story being told presents a number of interpretations
7   and should encourage imaginative character portraits to
8   emerge. It may be useful in the rehearsal period to
9   experiment with a performance metaphor for each
10   character. A metaphor is a figure of speech in which an
11   implied comparison is made between one thing and another
12   different thing. (Like Shakespeare's metaphor ' … all the
13   world's a stage.') You may also choose to observe the
14   behavioral patterns of others that might serve as role models
15   in the creation of real-life character portraits.
16
17
18 Man — unspecified   Male/Female
19 God — unspecified   Male/Female
20 Waiter — unspecified   Male/Female
21
22   *(In this dark comedy, Man bumps into God in a cheap, dimly-*
23   *lit café that is typical of the "no place" found in absurd plays.*
24   *They share some beer, eat some pretzels and talk about the*
25   *meaning of life and the mystery of the spiritual universe. Man*
26   *is not entirely satisfied that the meaning of life has been fully*
27   *answered. God is not entirely satisfied that the mystery of the*
28   *spiritual universe has been clearly understood.)*

1 MAN: Excuse me, but that's my pitcher of beer.

2 GOD: Oh, that's alright. I'm God.

3 MAN: You're God?

4 GOD: Quite right. *(He takes another pretzel)*

5 MAN: If you don't mind me saying so, you don't look like
6   God.

7 GOD: *(Looking directly at MAN for the first time)* Oh? And who
8   might you be, if I may ask?

9 MAN: I'm a man.

10 GOD: *(Giving him a look of careful appraisal)* Are you indeed?
11   Well, I'm afraid I'm not much impressed either.

12   *(MAN sits up and tries to straighten his rumpled suit.)*

13 MAN: I would have expected a deity to have better manners.

14 GOD: *(Smiling graciously)* Let's not quarrel, shall we? I just
15   dropped in here to relax. As for our expectations of one
16   another. Well, we are what we are, eh?

17   *(MAN is silent for a moment while GOD takes another sip of*
18   *beer.)*

19 MAN: Well, that's up to you, isn't it?

20 GOD: What?

21 MAN: We are what we are because you made us that way.

22 GOD: *(Sighs)* Oh dear. I gather that you are carrying the
23   usual load of human guilt and are searching for a
24   convenient place to dump it. Very well — you are what
25   I made you, so whatever it is, it's not your fault. Okay?
26   Now, let's enjoy our beer.

27   *(MAN, looking sullen, is silent again.)*

28 MAN: Look, I'm not trying to get out of anything. I accept
29   my responsibilities. It's just that if you're God, well,
30   you're more or less in charge of the whole thing, aren't
31   you? You have to take some of the responsibility, too.

32   *(GOD ignores him.)*

33   Anyway, it's my beer.

34 GOD: Oh, alright, alright. I'll buy the next pitcher. *(Aside)*
35   Or strike you dead.

1 MAN: You know, I've always wondered just exactly how the
2   responsibility should be divided. How much free will do
3   we really have, anyway?
4 GOD: Sorry. I'm not a philosopher.
5 MAN: But you're God!
6 GOD: Do you think that means I know everything? How
7   much free will do you suppose I have? Things are the
8   way they are. I'm God and you're a man, and neither of
9   us asked for it.
10 MAN: You mean you're not really in charge?
11 GOD: What, of everything? Every sparrow that falls and all
12   that? Well, technically, I suppose I am. But you can't
13   expect me to get personally involved in every little
14   detail. It's a big system, you know, and it generally rolls
15   along by itself without the need for much tinkering.
16 MAN: So you sit in cafes and drink beer.
17 GOD: I think the universe can spare me for a few hours.
18   What do you want me to do — dash around performing
19   one miracle after another, for centuries on end?
20 MAN: I'm not trying to tell you how to do your job. It just
21   seems to me that there are so many useful things you
22   could do.
23 GOD: Well, I like to be useful when I can, just like everyone
24   else. But as I said, it's a big system, and I have my
25   part in it, just as you have yours ...
26 MAN: *(Anxiously)* What is my part? What is my purpose?
27 GOD: *(Evasively)* Um, well, that's a little difficult ... I mean,
28   'purpose' and 'part' aren't exactly the same thing, so
29   I'm not sure ...
30 MAN: Purpose! What is my purpose?
31 GOD: Well. *(Pauses)* Well, strictly speaking, you don't
32   actually have a purpose. You're just here.
33 MAN: *(Rising from his chair)* No purpose? No purpose? No
34   meaning for my existence? You created a huge,
35   marvelous, inter-connected and ever-changing

1   universe, and you assigned no purpose to the most
2   intelligent life-form it contains?
3 GOD: Calm down, calm down. You're not the only one, you
4   know. I've never seen any sense in hermit crabs either,
5   but there they are. You mustn't take it personally.
6 MAN: So mankind has no more religious or philosophical
7   significance than hermit crabs?
8 GOD: *(Smiling brightly)* I'll bet that's a load off your mind,
9   isn't it?
10 MAN: No, no it's not. *(He sinks back into his chair)* Well,
11   that's it then, isn't it? Here we are, the intelligent apex
12   of creation, and there's nothing for us to do.
13 GOD: Oh, now, I didn't say that. There are lots of things for
14   you to do.
15 MAN: *(Glumly)* Such as?
16 GOD: Acquiring wealth and property, of course. And
17   fighting one another.
18 MAN: You talk as though greed and violence is all a jolly
19   game.
20 GOD: Certainly it's a game. And a very popular one, too. It
21   seems to satisfy most of your fellow mortals.
22 MAN: *(With excitement)* But you could change that!
23 GOD: *(Puzzled)* Could I? Hmm. But why would I want to?
24 MAN: Why? Why? To give us a reason for being, that's why.
25   To give mankind something to do besides killing one
26   another and piling up possessions. You could give
27   meaning to our existence.
28 GOD: *(Shrugging)* I don't see the point. You know, I've been
29   around for eons, and nobody has ever explained the
30   meaning of my existence. You shouldn't let it bother
31   you. Besides, you're talking about a rather large change
32   in the system, and that has all sorts of ramifications
33   that you haven't considered. It's really very difficult to
34   bring about that sort of change in the universe, except
35   by catastrophe.

1 MAN: Catastrophe?
2 GOD: You know — exploding stars, asteroids colliding with
3   planets — that sort of thing. You get complete
4   extermination of the existing species and a chance to
5   start all over again. Sometimes you even get new
6   planets — though sometimes you just get dust. But
7   anyway, you wouldn't want your little world to be
8   involved in something like that, would you? *(Aside)*
9   Though of course, it will be, sooner or later.
10 MAN: No, I suppose not, but there must be other ways.
11   What about evolution?
12 GOD: Ah, yes, evolution. You really can do some remarkable
13   things with evolution, over the course of a few million
14   years. But when you get right down to it, most of the
15   changes are superficial. The essential nature of the
16   beast is unaltered. Take your species, for example. You
17   started out as predatory apes, grouped together in small
18   bands that fought each other over territory. Haven't
19   really changed all that much, have you?
20   *(MAN looks helpless. He does not reply.)*
21   No, a whacking big chunk of rock, smashing into the
22   side of the planet — POW! *(He slams his fist into his
23   hand)* That's the way you get real changes.
24   *(MAN remains silent. GOD sips his beer and takes another
25   pretzel.)*
26 MAN: Well, scratch that idea, then.
27 GOD: Absolutely. Better to leave well enough alone, eh?
28   *(He peers into the bowl)* Do you think we can get some
29   more of these pretzels?
30 MAN: But if you can't make big changes, then how about
31   a few little ones? For example, why can't you make us
32   happy?
33 GOD: You have the means to make yourselves happy.
34 MAN: How?
35 GOD: *(Exasperated)* By acquiring possessions and fighting

1   one another — that's what makes you happy.

2 MAN: *(With contempt)* That's supposed to make us happy?
3   Well, let me tell you, it's not working worth a damn for
4   most of us.

5 GOD: Well, obviously, it can't work for everyone. I mean, if you
6   all had the same possessions, nobody would be happy,
7   would they? The point is to have more than everyone else.
8   And when two people fight, one can't win unless the other
9   is beaten. There is no joy without misery.

10 MAN: What kind of a screwy system is that? You haven't
11   even got the proportions right — ninety per cent of the
12   human race lives in poverty and oppression so that the
13   other ten per cent can enjoy wealth and power.

14 GOD: Things are as they are. *(He is cleaning up the last of the*
15   *pretzels)*

16 MAN: It's a disgrace! What kind of a way is this to run a
17   cosmos? Maybe if you you would just apply yourself —
18   and gimme that damn pretzel bowl! *(He snatches the bowl*
19   *away from GOD)* You could at least pay attention. You
20   never listen! For thousands of years, we've been sending
21   up prayers, incantations, hymns, burnt offerings — and
22   do you ever call back or drop us a note?

23 GOD: Actually, you've been a little slack on the burnt
24   offerings, lately.

25 MAN: That's not the point. Why won't you talk to us?

26 GOD: And the truth is, I'd rather have pretzels than burnt
27   offerings.

28 MAN: *(Furious)* To hell with the pretzels! Talk to me! If you
29   won't do anything, if you won't change anything, you
30   could at least talk to me! Let me know you exist!

31 GOD: Alright, alright. What do you want me to say?

32 MAN: I want you to tell me why things are as they are. And
33   why they can't be made better.

34 GOD: I never said things can't be better. But why are you
35   putting it all on me? It's your world as much as it is

1   mine. If it's dirty, abused, miserable, and hopeless,
2   what have you got to say about it?
3 MAN: *(Thinks for a second)* It was like that when I got here.
4 GOD: Oh sure, pass the buck. Look here, man, I know what
5   your problem is. When you were a young fellow, you
6   really thought that you would make things better, didn't
7   you? Thought you were pretty hot stuff. Thought you
8   would set the world on its ear. And now here you are,
9   twenty years later, and the world has set you on your
10   ear. Things didn't turn out as you expected, did they?
11   *(MAN says nothing.)*
12   *(Warming to his subject)* And now you'd like to know
13   whose fault it is. Why aren't you a genius? Why aren't
14   you famous? Why didn't your grand ideas and noble
15   ideals amount to anything? Why don't all the peoples
16   of the earth fall to their knees and worship you as the
17   great god-emperor who ended poverty, ignorance, and
18   disease? Or, to put it another way, why are you such a
19   poor, pitiful, worthless, impotent little schmuck?
20   *(MAN looks sadly into his beer, says nothing. GOD takes a*
21   *large swallow of beer and fixes MAN with a look of triumph*
22   *that quickly turns to pity.)*
23   Um ... got a bit carried away, didn't I? Look, I didn't
24   mean to say that you're not a perfectly good man ...
25 MAN: No, no. You're quite right. Most of my anger at the
26   world is really anger at myself, for not being more than
27   I am. *(Sighs)* But why is that, anyway? Couldn't you
28   just as easily have made me a genius as an impotent
29   little schmuck?
30 GOD: Well, it's a mass-production sort of thing, you know.
31   Most of you chaps come out about the same.
32 MAN: Ah.
33 GOD: Ah.
34   *(They sip their beer, silently.)*
35   *(Enter Waiter, with a dirty rag slung over his shoulder. He*

69

1 *begins clearing the table, making a big show of having to*
2 *gather up the discarded newspaper, while giving dirty looks*
3 *to GOD and MAN, who remain indifferent. Then he wipes the*
4 *table with his rag and picks up GOD's beer glass.)*
5 **Wait. I'm not finished with that.**
6 **WAITER:** *(Slams the glass back on the table)* **Huh. Never**
7 **finished with anything, are you?**
8 **GOD: Oh, don't start with me tonight. Go and fetch us**
9 **some more pretzels.** *(He pushes the empty bowl into*
10 *Waiter's stomach, so that the Waiter is forced to take it)*
11 **WAITER:** *(Dropping the bowl on the table)* **You ain't the boss**
12 **around here, no matter what some people might think.**
13 **MAN:** *(Appalled at this display of disrespect)* **Hey, do you know**
14 **who you're talking to?**
15 **WAITER: Sure, I know who I'm talking to. That's God. Big**
16 **deal. But I ain't seen you in here before.**
17 **GOD: He's a friend of mine. A man. I would say a man like**
18 **you, but he isn't nearly as ignorant or ill-mannered as**
19 **you.**
20 **WAITER:** *(Squints at MAN)* **You call that a man? Look at him**
21 **— confused, useless. A jumble of mismatched parts. If**
22 **I was God and couldn't make a better man than that,**
23 **I'd pack it in.**
24 **GOD: Yes, well, fortunately for all of us, I am God and you**
25 **are a waiter. So do your job and go away.** *(He makes the*
26 *Waiter take the pretzel bowl again)*
27 **WAITER: Huh. And what job do I have to do? Just the same**
28 **old stuff, over and over again, ain't it?**
29 **GOD:** *(Rolling His eyes)* **I've already had this conversation**
30 **once today.**
31 **WAITER:** *(Ignoring GOD)* **Yep, it's the same old stuff. Just**
32 **like that guy, Sisyphus, you get to rolling that stone up**
33 **that mountain. It rolls right back down and he's got to**
34 **start all over. Just like the rest of us.**
35 **GOD: No. The difference between Sisyphus and you is that**

1   he doesn't whine all the time.

2 WAITER: Maybe that's because he's immortal. At least he
3   ain't just waiting around to die.

4 GOD: It seems to me you should be grateful for your
5   mortality. Few men find life so good that they want it
6   to last forever.

7 WAITER: And who's fault is that?

8 GOD: I assure you, I haven't the slightest idea.

9   *(WAITER gives GOD a look of utter contempt, then exits*
10   *slowly carrying the pretzel bowl and muttering to himself.)*

11 WAITER: Huh. Call yourself a God. Huh.

12 MAN: Do you have to put up with that sort of thing often?

13 GOD: What do you mean?

14 MAN: I mean the way that fellow talked to you. He showed
15   no respect.

16 GOD: Do you suppose I care? I'm God, not a gang leader.
17   The respect of men is of no consequence to me.

18 MAN: So religion is of no importance?

19 GOD: You do have a wonderful faculty for jumping to
20   conclusions. I said nothing of the kind. Religion may
21   not matter much to me, but it is of immense
22   importance to mankind.

23 MAN: But if you don't care about it, why should we? Why
24   should we even believe in you? Many people don't, you
25   know.

26 GOD: True, but everyone believes in something. *(He fixes*
27   *MAN with his gaze)* What do you believe in?
28   Reincarnation? Science? Logic? The progress of
29   civilization? I know there must be something.
30   Everyone's life is sufficiently terrible to require some
31   sort of self-delusion.

32 MAN: I ... I believe in a sense of order. There must be
33   reasons for things.

34 GOD: Ah, order and reason. How marvelous. You are
35   probably a bit disappointed by reality, then, aren't you?

1   MAN: Well, it does seem to me you could run a tighter ship.
2   GOD: Yes, I suppose it does. You'd like everything to be
3   under control at all times. No accidents. Bad things
4   would only happen to bad people, and good things to
5   good people. Cosmic justice, right? And as you said
6   earlier, life should have meaning. Everyone should know
7   the reason for his existence, so that he would know
8   what he is supposed to do. Yes, who can deny the
9   attraction of such ideas? Lots of people choose to
10   believe that that's exactly the way things are. *(GOD
11   leans close to MAN and speaks with great intensity)* **The
12   idea of a chaotic universe, a universe without remorse,
13   hope, or pity is altogether too terrifying for you, isn't it?**
14 MAN: *(Shaken)* Well, that can't be how it is, can it? Such a
15   universe would have no God, and here you are.
16 GOD: *(Grinning wickedly)* **Am I?** 'If God did not exist, it
17   would be necessary to invent him.' Voltaire wasn't the
18   first to think of that. You humans have been
19   manufacturing gods for ages. Some cultures turned out
20   a couple of dozen. I tell you, it keeps a fellow hopping,
21   answering to all those different names.
22 MAN: Well, if you don't like it, you could straighten people
23   out easily enough.
24 GOD: Who says I don't like it? It's very convenient to have
25   a hundred different identities. It gives a fellow scope.
26 MAN: Do you mean you adjust your behavior according to
27   our expectations?
28 GOD: Not necessarily. I just mean that when you have
29   multiple personalities, things always seem to be going
30   your way — for one of you, at least. Take the Middle
31   East. When the Jews beat the Arabs in battle, they
32   thank Yahweh. When the Arabs win one, they praise
33   Allah. Can't lose, can I?
34 MAN: *(Grimly)* I would think you'd want to put an end to
35   things like that.

1   GOD: *(Sighing)* **You really don't understand me. That's**
2   **quite alright, of course. No one does. But you take it**
3   **far too seriously. Loosen up, old man. Stop worrying**
4   **about things that you can't possibly do anything about.**
5   **The world, you must admit, is not an altogether**
6   **horrible place. Why don't you pay a bit more attention**
7   **to beauty, pleasure, and a good glass of beer?** *(He lifts*
8   *his mug in a salute to MAN)* **After all, if you're going to**
9   **blame me for all the world's ills, the least you can do**
10   **is give me credit for the good things as well.**
11 MAN: *(Apologetically)* **Yes, I know I should. I try. I don't**
12   **mean to be unappreciative. But perhaps you don't**
13   **understand us. It's very difficult to be mortal, you**
14   **know. When you think about death, you can't help but**
15   **take life seriously.**
16 GOD: **Couldn't disagree more. Thinking about death is a**
17   **damned good reason not to take life seriously — at**
18   **least, not too seriously. As I once said to Camus, 'The**
19   **fact that life is absurd is no reason not to have a good**
20   **lunch. It's a reason to ask for extra portions.'** *(He fills*
21   *MAN's beer mug while MAN watches silently)* **Come on,**
22   **cheer up. You ought to try to laugh a little.**
23 MAN: **What is there to laugh at?**
24 GOD: **Yourself. Your friends. Your situation. Think cosmic.**
25   **Act cosmic. That's my advice.**
26 MAN: *(Sighs)* **That's easier said than done.**
27 GOD: **Of course it is. Humor takes great courage. A brave**
28   **man is a man who can laugh in the face of the Devil —**
29   **or God.**
30 MAN: **Perhaps I'm not a brave man. I never wanted to be**
31   **brave, anyway. I only wanted to be good. Do you have**
32   **to be brave to be good?**
33 GOD: **You do ask the damnedest questions. But why**
34   **should you want to be good? Do you think it matters**
35   **to me? Because it absolutely does not. Saint or sinner.**

1   It's all one to me.

2 **MAN:** *(Smiling weakly)* They say virtue is its own reward.

3 **GOD:** That's why virtue is unpopular. Most people want a

4   tangible reward. Or they at least want some sort of

5   special sign from me.

6 **MAN:** Maybe they just want to know that you exist. Is that

7   too much to expect?

8 **GOD:** *(Looking closely at MAN)* I'm afraid it is. If you truly

9   believe that virtue is its own reward, then you must also

10   believe in me. Otherwise, there's no point, is there? You

11   have faith, old man, and faith does not require proof.

12 **MAN:** *(Anxiously)* Yes. Yes, I do have faith. I have to have

13   faith, because there is nothing else. But why is it so

14   terribly hard to have faith? Isn't faith supposed to bring

15   peace of mind?

16 **GOD:** Peace of mind is achieved only when you know that

17   all your sins have been forgiven. And when you are able

18   to forgive the sins of everyone else — even those of God

19   Himself.

20 **MAN:** But it's so hard! So hard!

21 **GOD:** *(Softly)* **Never mind that.** *(He closes his hand over*

22   *MAN's hand)* **For now, it's enough to know that you are**

23   **not alone.**

24

25

26

27

28

29

30

31

32

33

34

35

VOICES OF SPIRIT AND SOUL

Voices of Spirit and Soul

The voices of spirit and soul add a new flavor and texture of directness and simplicity in an audition. The characters are common men, women, and young adults who express universal human qualities while often at odds with present-day society. They explore the outer limits of suffering with a healthy measure of courage and determination, in spite of the fact that there is no apparent means of escape for them. The characters frequently struggle to preserve personal values, as a means of expressing their basic human dignity. They confront current issues to arouse our deeper emotions so that we may also examine our life more objectively.

In playing these voices, you should pay attention to imagery, language and word choice to better understand a character's action, attitude, or mood. Look for subtle physical actions, personal traits, mannerisms, behavior patterns, or gestures that help define each character. Your reality-based performance blueprint should also include a detailed analysis of the character's emotional or psychological state-of-mind. Look for the "inner truth" of these characters and convey that truth in a direct, simple manner. When you visualize your "self" and your own "life" in these characters, your audition will bear witness to the voices of spirit and soul.

Fires in the Mirror
by Anna Deavere Smith

1	Girl — age unspecified	Female

2

3 *(An African-American girl looks in the mirror and reflects on*
4 *her life. Her observations crackle with humorous glimpses of*
5 *herself and her Hispanic school classmates. This script is one*
6 *in a series of interviews drawn from the 1991 riots in the*
7 *Crown Heights section of Brooklyn, New York — after a young*
8 *African-American child was killed by a car in a rabbi's*
9 *motorcade and a Jewish student was slain in retaliation.)*

10

11 **When I look in the mirror ...**
12 **I don't know.**
13 **How did I find out I was Black ...**
14 **(Tongue sound)**
15 **When I grew up and I look in the mirror and saw I was**
16 **Black.**
17 **When I look at my parents,**
18 **That's how I knew I was Black.**
19 **Look at my skin.**
20 **You Black?**
21 **Black is beautiful.**
22 **I don't know.**
23 **That's what I always say.**
24 **I think White is beautiful too.**
25 **But I think Black is beautiful too.**
26 **In my class nobody is White, everybody's Black,**
27 **and some of them is Hispanic.**
28 **In my class**
29 **you can't call any of them Puerto Ricans.**

1	They despise Puerto Ricans, I don't know why.
2	They think that Puerto Ricans are stuck up and
3	everything.
4	They say, Oh My Gosh my nail broke, look at that
5	cute guy and everything.
6	But they act like that themselves.
7	They act just like White girls.
8	Black girls is not like that.
9	Please, you should be in my class.
10	Like they say that Puerto Ricans act like that
11	and they don't see that they act like that themselves.
12	Black girls, they do bite off the Spanish girls,
13	they bite off of your clothes.
14	You don't know what that means? biting off?
15	Like biting off somebody's clothes
16	Like Cop, following,
17	and last year they used to have a lot of girls like that.
18	They come to school with a style, right?
19	And if they see another girl with that style?
20	Oh my gosh look at her.
21	What she think she is,
22	she tryin' to bite off of me in some way
23	no don't be bitin' off my sneakers
24	or like that.
25	Or doin' a hair style
26	I mean Black people are into hair styles.
27	So they come to school, see somebody with a certain
28	style,
29	they say uh-huh I'm gonna get me one just like that
30	un-huh,
31	that's the way Black people are
32	Yea-ah!
33	They don't like people doing that to them
34	and they do that to other people,
35	so the Black girls will follow the Spanish girls.

1   The Spanish girls don't bite off of us.
2   Some of the Black girls follow them.
3   But they don't mind.
4   They don't care.
5   They follow each other.
6   Like there's three girls in my class,
7   they from the Dominican Republic.
8   They all stick together like glue.
9   They all three best friends.
10 They don't follow nobody,
11 like there's none of them lead or anything.
12 They don't hang around us either.
13 They're
14 by themselves.
15
16
17
18
19
20
21
22
23
24
25
26
27
28
29
30
31
32
33
34
35

R. A. W., 'Cause I'm a Woman
by Diana Son

1   Unspecified   Female

2

3   *(A single Asian female is stranded in an empty gulf between*
4   *different cultures. Here, she offers a sensitive look at what it*
5   *means to live in a society that is torn between reality and*
6   *racial stereotypes. Her intimate feelings of a woman fighting*
7   *to survive in the urban jungle are voiced in strong, sometimes*
8   *spirited, language. She refuses, however, to surrender her*
9   *sense of pride.)*

10

11   **A beautiful woman should never have to beg for the**
12   **love of a man but I. Have begged because I. Am not**
13   **beautiful outside. No I know. They called me paleface**
14   **when I was a child. Not just to tease me because I was**
15   **Chinese because I was Japanese because I was**
16   **KoreanThaiVietnamese all rolled up into one no I know.**
17   **My face is flat and truly flat when I was a child. And**
18   **company came we ate store bought desserts off of white**
19   **china dishes. They measured seven inches across seven**
20   **inches up and down and sneaking one into the bathroom**
21   **I put one up to my face and seven inches all around it fit**
22   **me. The plate fit my face like a glove. And my eyes are**
23   **squinty. Small not almond shaped like the pretty geishas**
24   **but slits like papercuts tiny. My hair is straight flat not**
25   **shiny like the girl on the macadamia nut bottle but dry I**
26   **got a perm it helps but I hate the smell. I have trouble**
27   **finding men you're not surprised. No I know. I took an ad**
28   **out in the personal ads Single Asian Female looking for**
29   **Single Man of any race to love to care for to share**

1   bountiful joy with. Will answer all replies. I got a jillion
2   replies a bouquet of hopeful suitors. I answered them all
3   I said I would. It took days I found some nice ones. I
4   arranged to meet them at convenient times in attractive
5   places. The men came but they wore disappointed faces.
6   I said I never promised you I was pretty. They said you
7   said you were Asian — I assumed. I forgave them these
8   men who were not so cute themselves. I held no grudge.
9   I let them off the hook. Outside I am ugly. No I know. But
10   I am beautiful in my heart yes God knows my heart is the
11   home of great love. These men weren't beautiful inside
12   or out. I missed nothing. I don't feel bad. This beautiful
13   woman will never beg.
14
15
16
17
18
19
20
21
22
23
24
25
26
27
28
29
30
31
32
33
34
35

In Violence We Trust
by Gus Edwards

1 Joanie — late twenties   Female
2
3   *(Joanie, a grade school teacher in her late twenties, extols the*
4   *virtues of Dr. Martin Luther King, Jr. in this stirring tribute to*
5   *the late civil rights activist. Although Joanie didn't know Dr.*
6   *King personally, she read his books, contributed money to his*
7   *causes and felt outrage when he was spat upon and called*
8   *derogatory names. Now, she celebrates his struggle and*
9   *serves as a witness to his loss.)*
10
11   **Didn't we know what we were doing? Didn't we know that**
12   **this was a great man passing through our midst? ... I**
13   **recall a speech I made to my class one day, saying in**
14   **effect that from time to time we are visited by**
15   **greatness. Or have 'greatness' thrust upon us. That**
16   **great men exist right now and right here. But we're**
17   **so used to reading about them in history books we**
18   **refuse to believe or accept that they could be living in**
19   **our country and in our time. 'In India maybe or in the**
20   **Far East, perhaps. But here, in America? Give me a**
21   **break.' ... My seventh graders of course didn't**
22   **understand what I was talking about. But I was talking**
23   **about him. About Martin Luther King Jr. The man**
24   **America killed because it was threatened by his**
25   **greatness.**
26   **They said he was standing on a balcony when the**
27   **fatal shot was fired. What he was doing there has never**
28   **been satisfactorily explained. They said he was out there**
29   **taking the air. That's reasonable enough. Innocent**

enough, unless you're a black man trying to better the condition of your people in America. Then you're embarking on a dangerous interlude. For White America doesn't want her darker brethren reaching after equality. She wants things to remain the same. Forever and ever the same. And anything or anyone who comes along and tries to change that pattern makes her angry. Very angry. Violently angry. And that's when the bullets fly. We can never be sure about anything. Never be confident about anything until we let the bullets fly. Then we're happy. Then we're fine. Then we're American, once again. The only problem is: Somebody has to pay the price. First it was him. But one day it's sure to be — you.

My Death
by Martha Hoos

1   Unspecified   Male/Female
2
3   *(An heroic figure, dressed in white, addresses the questions*
4   *of death and immortality from an unusual point of view.*
5   *There is a reminder here of the promise of eternal happiness*
6   *for those who truly believe in the power of redemption. The*
7   *character portrait is brought into sharp focus when it is*
8   *revealed that the mysterious figure is sketching a spiritual*
9   *rather than physical death.)*
10
11 I died last night. No, I did, really. I am dead. It was
12 weird, dying I mean. I've never died before. It was scary,
13 but not as scary as you'd think. At first it was, but after
14 I decided to take that eternal plunge I was so full of
15 energy. I felt like the Energizer Bunny. It was
16 exhilarating. That's strange, huh? I used to wonder what
17 happened when you died. I mean do you just die and
18 cease to exist, or do you have a soul? If you do have a
19 soul, where do you go? Is there really a heaven and a
20 hell? Well, now I know the answer. There is life after
21 death and there is a heaven and a hell. You might be
22 wondering how I died. It was really gruesome and
23 painful. It was the worst way a person could die. I died
24 on a cross, with a man named Jesus. You see it wasn't
25 a physical death I died last night. It was a spiritual
26 death. I placed all my sin on Jesus and He washed my
27 soul clean. I had never felt so pure or high or peaceful
28 and calm or WHOLE. Jesus filled this emptiness inside
29 me. If you haven't died yet you feel what I'm talking

1   about. It's like this big black emptiness that just
2   consumes you. Consumes your life. You're depressed
3   and morbid. But you don't want to say that you're
4   depressed because depressed people are losers who
5   have no control of their life. I used to be so morbid that
6   my motto was 'everyone was born to die' or 'once you're
7   born, you start dying.' It's still my motto, but now the
8   meaning has changed. I believe that once we are born
9   our lives lead us to die in Christ. I guess you'd have to
10 die to know what I mean. I suggest you try it. It will be
11 the best decision you'll ever make. I guarantee it.
12
13
14
15
16
17
18
19
20
21
22
23
24
25
26
27
28
29
30
31
32
33
34
35

The Colour of Justice
by Richard Norton-Taylor

1   Duwayne — age unspecified   Male

3   *(This is a dramatic reconstruction of the 1999 public hearings*

4   *that erupted into national outrage in London, England when*

5   *black teenager Stephen Lawrence was stabbed to death by a*

6   *gang of white youths and the police investigation failed to*

7   *convict the alleged criminals. Here, Duwayne Brooks, who*

8   *was with Stephen Lawrence when he was attacked, talks of*

9   *their friendship and the events leading up to the murder.)*

11   **Stephen Lawrence was one of my best friends. We met**

12   **on our first day of secondary school — the Blackheath**

13   **Bluecoats Church of England School. Both Stephen and**

14   **I were 18 when Steve was murdered. We saw each other**

15   **regularly ... In the evening we were hurrying to get home**

16   **as soon as possible. We were just looking for a bus on**

17   **Well-Hall Road. We were attacked by a group of white**

18   **boys, one of whom shouted, 'What, what nigger?' I can't**

19   **bear to go into the details ... As we were running from**

20   **the attack, Steve fell to the ground. I stopped on the**

21   **pavement. I went back and bent down and looked at**

22   **him. He was lying by a tree. He was still breathing. He**

23   **could not speak. I saw his blood running away.**

24   **I ran across to the phone box and dialed 999 ... I**

25   **was pacing up and down, up and down. I was desperate**

26   **for the ambulance. It was taking too long. I was**

27   **frightened by the amount of blood Steve was losing. I**

28   **saw his life fading away. I didn't know what to do to help**

29   **him. I was frightened I would do something wrong. WPC**

Bethel said, 'How did it start? Did they chase you for nothing?' I said one of them shouted, 'What, what nigger?' She asked me if I had any weapons on me. She was treating me like she was suspicious of me, not like she wanted to help. If she had asked me of more details of the boys' descriptions or what they were wearing I would have told her. Those would have been sensible questions. None of the uniformed officers were doing anything for Steve. They just stood there doing nothing.

The ambulance arrived. They carried Steve to the ambulance on a stretcher. His unopened ginger beer can fell from him on the floor. I picked it up. I took it home and kept it in my room, until one day it exploded. I am told I called the police 'pigs' ... I did not. I don't use those words. I was driven to Plumstead police station. I now know that in their statements the police said I broke a window in the front office. I didn't. I wasn't even in the front office. It just shows they were treating me like a criminal and not like a victim. They kept saying, are you sure they said 'What, what nigger?' I said, 'I'm telling the truth.' The senior officer said, 'You mean you have done nothing to provoke them in any way?' I said, 'No, we were just waiting for a bus.'

Accepting Death
by Kimberly A. McCormick

1   Young woman   Female

2

3   *(Saddened by the death of her grandmother, a young woman*

4   *reminisces about growing up and spending time with her*

5   *kind and generous family matriarch. She contemplates the*

6   *meaning of life and death, as well as what lies beyond the*

7   *grave. Though grieving, she learns to appreciate the little*

8   *things in life. Feeling the spirit of her grandmother, she finds*

9   *new joy and meaning in the world.)*

10

11   Why is it that people have to die? I just don't get it. It

12   seems as if people who spend their entire life caring

13   about others should be allowed to live forever.

14   My grandmother died today. She was ninety-nine,

15   and I truly believed she would live forever. In my heart

16   she still does live on. There has to be more to this world

17   than just this, doesn't there? I have to believe she's in

18   a heaven someplace so special where she will always be

19   healthy and happy.

20   She told me not to grieve for her after she was gone.

21   She said that it was time for her to go to a much better

22   place, where she would never feel pain or heartache

23   again. I'm trying hard to do what she asked me to do,

24   but it's so hard. I miss her so much.

25   When I was little my sisters and I took turns staying

26   overnight at my grandma's apartment. I loved the

27   licorice candy she kept in her glass jar. It was wrapped

28   in shiny silver paper and brought out only for us.

29   We loved to sit and play Pick-Up Sticks with her.

1   Somehow I always won. When I became an adult and my
2   own children would play this game with Grandma, I
3   suddenly realized that Grandma always lets the children
4   win!
5   Grandma worked in a rescue mission house. She
6   spent her entire life helping people who were having hard
7   times. It was her religion that kept her brave, her belief
8   that God is real and that he was always with her.
9   Everyone at the mission respected my grandma. It
10   doesn't seem right that she's gone.
11   My whole outlook on life has changed now. When
12   Grandma was alive I didn't even think about death. It
13   was something I knew happened all around me, but
14   never to someone I knew. Now, I've learned to
15   appreciate every day I'm alive. We never know when it
16   will be our turn to pass on from this world.
17   Grandma's death taught me to look around for the
18   little things in life that can bring joy. I try to look for the
19   bright side of things. I used to be upset when I had to
20   go to work, now I'm thankful I have a job. When a storm
21   comes that ruins my plans, I know that plans can be
22   changed and the sun will eventually come out again.
23   It's funny how death changes a person. I feel like
24   Grandma is looking down on me from heaven, helping
25   me to understand that my life has a purpose, and it's
26   my responsibility to figure out what it is and do it.
27   *(The next line is said looking upward.)* I'm **trying,**
28   Grandma. I really am. I think I finally understand what
29   you meant when you said, "Life's not easy, but it is
30   worthwhile."
31
32
33
34
35

Twirler
by Jane Martin

1   April — young adult   Female
2
3   *(A young woman, dressed in a spangled, one-piece swimsuit,*
4   *stands Center Stage. Holding a shining silver baton in her*
5   *hand, she shares an intimate glimpse of the pleasure — as*
6   *well as the pain — in the life of a "twirler." The character*
7   *portrait blends a good helping of spirit and soul to help guide*
8   *wiser young women, or men, through the maze of grim*
9   *battlefield competition.)*
10
11   I started when I was six. Momma sawed off a broom
12   handle, and Uncle Carbo slapped some sort of silver
13   paint, well, gray, really, on it and I went down in the
14   basement and twirled. Later on Momma hit the daily
15   double on horses named Spin Dry and Silver Revolver
16   and she said that was a sign so she gave me lessons at
17   the Dainty Deb Dance Studio, where the lady, Miss
18   Aurelia, taught some twirling on the side.
19   I won the Ohio Juniors title when I was six and the
20   Midwest Young Adult Division three years later, and
21   then in high school I finished fourth in the nationals.
22   Momma and I wore look-alike Statue of Liberty
23   costumes that she had to send clear to Nebraska to get,
24   and Daddy was there in a T-shirt with my name, April —
25   my first name is April and my last name is March. There
26   were four thousand people there, and when they yelled
27   my name golden balloons fell out of the ceiling. Nobody,
28   not even Charlene Ann Morrison, ever finished fourth at
29   my age.

1   Oh, I've flown high and known tragedy, both. My
2   daddy says it's put spirit in my soul and steel in my
3   heart. My left hand was crushed in a riding accident by
4   a horse named Big Blood Red, and though I came back
5   to twirl, I couldn't do it at the highest level. That was
6   denied me by Big Blood Red, who clipped my wings. You
7   mustn't pity me, though. Oh, by no means! Being
8   denied showed me the way, showed me the glory that
9   sits inside life where you can't see it.

10   One time I was doing fire batons at a night game,
11   and all of a sudden I see this guy walk out of the stands.
12   I was doing triples and he walks right out past the half-
13   time marshals, comes up to me — he had this blue
14   bead headband, I can still see it. Walks right up, and
15   when I come front after a back reverse he spits in my
16   face. That's the only, single time I ever dropped a baton.
17   Dropped 'em both in front of sixty thousand people. And
18   he smiles, see, and he says this thing I won't repeat. He
19   called me a bodily part in front of half of Ohio!

20   You haven't twirled, have you? I can see that by your
21   hands. Would you like to hold my silver baton? Here, hold
22   it. You can't imagine what it feels like to have that baton
23   up in the air. I used to twirl with that baton up in the air.
24   I used to twirl with this girl who called it blue-collar Zen.
25   The 'tons catch the sun when they're up, and when they
26   go up, you go up, too. You can't twirl if you're not 'inside'
27   the 'ton. When you've got 'em up over twenty feet, it's like
28   flying or gliding. Your hands are still down, but your
29   insides spin and rise and leave the ground.

30   The secret for a twirler is the light. You live or die
31   with the lights. It's your fate. The best is a February sky
32   clouded right over in the late afternoon. It's all
33   background then, and what happens is that the 'tons
34   leave tracks, traces, they etch the air, and if you're hot,
35   if your hands have it, you can draw on the sky.

1   God, Charlene Ann Morrison. Charlene Ann! She was
2   inspired by something beyond man. She won the
3   nationals nine years in a row. Unparalleled and
4   unrepeatable. The last two years she had leukemia and
5   at the end you could see through her hands when she
6   twirled. Charlene Ann died with a 'ton thirty feet up, her
7   momma swears on that. I roomed with Charlene at a
8   regional in Fargo, and she may have been fibbin', but
9   she said there was a day when her 'tons erased while
10   they turned. Like the sky was a sheet of rain and the
11   'tons were car wipers and when she had erased this
12   certain part of the sky you could see the face of Lord
13   God Jesus, and His hair was all rhinestones and He was
14   doing this incredible singing like the sound of a piccolo.
15   The people who said that Charlene was crazy probably
16   never twirled a day in their life.
17   Twirling is the physical parallel of revelation. You
18   can't know that. Twirling is the throwing of yourself up
19   to God. It's a pure gift, hidden from Satan because it is
20   wrapped and disguised in the midst of football. It is God-
21   throwing, spirit fire, and very few come to it. You have to
22   grow eyes in your heart to understand its message, and
23   when it opens to you it becomes your path to suffer
24   ridicule, to be crucified by misunderstanding, and to be
25   spit upon. I need my baton now.
26   There is one twirling no one sees. At the winter
27   solstice we got to a meadow God showed us just outside
28   of Green Bay. The God-throwers come there on
29   December twenty-first. There's snow. Sometimes deep
30   snow, and our clothes fall away, and we stand
31   unprotected while acolytes bring the 'tons. They are
32   ebony 'tons with razors set all along the shaft. They are
33   three feet long. One by one the twirlers throw, two 'tons
34   each, thirty feet up, and as they fall back they cut your
35   hands. The razors arch into the air and find God and

1 then fly down to take your blood in a crucifixion, and the
2 red drops draw God on the ground, and if you are up
3 with the batons you can look down and see Him
4 revealed. Red on white. Red on white. You can't imagine.
5 You can't imagine how wonderful that is.
6   I started twirling when I was six, but I never really
7 twirled until my hand was crushed by the horse named
8 Big Blood Red. I have seen God's face from thirty feet
9 up in the air, and I know Him. Listen. I will leave my
10 silver baton here for you. Lying here as if I forgot it. And
11 when the people file out you can wait back and pick it
12 up. It can be yours. It can be your burden. It is the eye
13 of the needle. I leave it for you.
14
15
16
17
18
19
20
21
22
23
24
25
26
27
28
29
30
31
32
33
34
35

"Tassie Suffers"
adapted from *Claptrap*
by Ken Friedman

1   Tassie — late twenties   Female
2
3   *(Tassie, an aspiring actress in her twenties, meets a friend in*
4   *a coffee shop and confesses that her recent audition has been*
5   *a fiasco. This riotous look at a madcap actress features all the*
6   *theatrical tricks and taboos familiar to aspiring actors*
7   *everywhere. There is delicious mischief in Tassie's eccentric*
8   *behavior, and that gives a sense of reality to the incredible*
9   *events that unfold.)*
10
11   My day? You want to hear about my day? No, you don't!
12   Does anyone really give a damn about my day? No! But
13   you asked! So, okay, I'll tell you. Today, I spent three
14   and a half hours on line waiting for another audition. I
15   know, I know ... But, it was for this daring, new avant-
16   garde theatre group that was going to do *The Cherry*
17   *Orchard* in a totally wild way. Outdoors in a real forest.
18   Yes! And everyone gets to chop down a tree! Hey, I
19   went. And there must have been over a hundred actors
20   in line, several with sharpened axes. Why didn't I think
21   of that? All I had on was a peasant apron, my red
22   babushka, and heavy boots. But, I looked terrific. For
23   what? Because, just as I'm nearing the head of the line,
24   just when I'm up to my ass in emotional borscht, the
25   word came out: THEY CHANGED THE PLAY! You heard
26   me. Changed it! Four from the door and it was now an
27   untitled comedy about a vegetable market in Trenton,
28   New Jersey. Is that stupid? But, there were three roles
29   for women. A ghetto teen: tough, but who secretly

1   reads Plato; an aging produce woman who once had an
2   affair with Fidel Castro (remember him?); and an
3   oversexed librarian who loves young boys more than she
4   loves old books. When I read that list, I flipped. I'm right
5   for all of them! But, now I'm still wearing my boots. I'm
6   screwed! 'Next!' I go in. 'Okay, Tassie, do you know the
7   roles that are open? Three women. Good. Honey, relax.
8   Take a few moments ... and improvise.' 'Huh? Improvise
9   what?' 'Improvise. We want to see what you can come
10   up with. Be free. Have fun. Enjoy.'

11   Have fun? Enjoy? You nitwit! Have you been
12   standing in line since Tuesday? My throat is dry. My
13   hands are wet. And who the hell am I supposed to be?
14   The tomato-selling Cubaphile, the philosophic juvenile,
15   or the oversexed pedophile? They waited. I waited. And
16   then it happened. I exploded. I burst into the greatest
17   single audition ever given anywhere by anyone! I was all
18   three at once! A Cuban cashier telling an eight year old
19   to shut his mouth in the public library! And then I was
20   a New Jersey dictator stealing fruit from an aging
21   teenager who wanted more from life than papayas and
22   apples! And more! And more! I went up, down, in and
23   out and beyond in an incredible torrent of amazingly
24   perfect choices. Weeping, dancing, loving, and walking
25   as three people at once! Acting? Ha! Above acting.
26   Fission, baby! I flared! I seared! I was fire.

27   And when it was all over I stood panting in a silence
28   that deserves to be called: enchanted. I waited. My head
29   bowed. And finally, one of them, a man who looked sort
30   of worried, said: 'Thank you ... very ... interesting ... '

31   Interesting? Is the Venus DeMilo interesting?

32   'Thank you, uh ... Miss Manson. Do you need your
33   picture?'

34   And so I left. Again. I walked out ... But, I was great!
35   They may not know it, because they measure me

1 against themselves. But, I know what I did. And so do
2 you. And as of today, I am special! No matter what they
3 say! I mean, what the hell do those murderers know? So,
4 of course, well now I am a little let down. A little
5 depressed. But, I'll be fine. God. So, that was my day.
6 Okay, now how the hell was yours?
7
8
9
10
11
12
13
14
15
16
17
18
19
20
21
22
23
24
25
26
27
28
29
30
31
32
33
34
35

Perfection
by Deanna Riley Cain

1   Roxy — adult   Female

2

3   *(Roxy, a slightly large and sophisticated woman, is offended*

4   *when she observes someone staring at her from a distance.*

5   *Pausing, abruptly, in her idle routine, Roxy gives a festive*

6   *color to her chatter about the role of "denial" in helping to*

7   *achieve a sense of perfection. Her social commentary is*

8   *properly served, the wit sharp and the message delicious!)*

9

10   I am perfect. I know what you're thinking ... But you're

11   wrong. I'm right. Don't worry. Happens all the time.

12   Despite what most people think, you're not born perfect.

13   Born with a silver spoon, born on third base, born again,

14   but not born perfect. I was making myself miserable.

15   Everywhere I looked, I was wrong. Wasn't thin enough,

16   tan enough, sexy enough, smart enough, dumb enough.

17   Miserable. Miserable. Miserable. Couldn't cook, clean, or

18   macrame holiday placemats. Couldn't balance a

19   checkbook or do math homework. My doctors were out

20   of network, my cell phone was out of range, and my

21   computer was out of disc space. My grocery line was the

22   longest, my ATM was jammed, and my dog had fleas.

23   Again. My Christmas cards were never addressed,

24   written, or mailed. But I did buy the cards. My favorite

25   ice cream is vanilla. Plain vanilla. Not even French

26   vanilla. I was a 'C' student. Sometimes I would get a

27   'C+.' Average with extra effort. Not perfect. Not even a

28   perfect failure. Average. And I wanted a change. I

29   wanted to be on the 'A-list.' No waiting at crowded

restaurants. Tellers open their windows just for me. Always having exact change. But how to make me change? Where to look? How to start?

Then it came to me. Denial. Denial was the perfect strategy. Now I can't claim credit for it because I wasn't perfect at the time. My mother gave me the insight. My mother has always had a fabulous figure, not perfect mind you, but very good. Much better than mine to tell you the truth. Quite voluptuous. As she has gotten a little older, she has put on a few pounds and is not the size she used to be. But does she acknowledge that? Not for one second. My mother explained to me that she is wearing larger sizes because sizes were originally designed around 1906 and American women were smaller then. As advances in medicine, diet, and exercise have progressed, American women have grown in size. So the fashion designers all over the world got together to make adjustments in sizes. Although she 'wears' a fourteen or sixteen, she 'is' still a size six. The sizes got smaller and it's because of the fashion designers' international conspiracy. My mother is a very happy woman. She believes she is the same size she was when she was twenty-two. Ignorance is bliss. Denial is the way to happiness.

At first, I had a little trouble working in the denial. At the bank, I cut in front of a six-foot-two, 210-pound woman. Lesson one: Pick your denials carefully. The next time, I pictured myself in the front of the line and everyone in front of me was performance art. Very entertaining. No stress. They actually paid me to see the performance. What more could I want? Then the perfection started rolling. My steaks were actually cooked medium rare and not something in between. The ATM gave me an extra twenty. Got the cheapest long distance coverage. Bought placemats. Balanced my

1   checkbook. Got a raise. Got two. Had groceries
2   delivered at home. Won a new computer. Dumped my
3   old cell phone. My dog's fleas left him for another dog.
4   Felt taller, thinner, sexier. And I started wearing pre-
5   fashion-conspiracy sizes. Vanilla was the flavor of the
6   week — for a month. Finally, I had achieved perfection.
7   Bliss.
8   There's only one impediment to total worldwide
9   perfection. I need you to help acknowledge that I'm
10   perfect. 'Duchess of Perfection. Queen of Denial.' *(Raises*
11   *voice)* While I reign supreme, everyone will be happy.
12   Perfection in every pot. Denial at every door. 'Queen for
13   a Day every day.' What a success story. A 'C' is an 'A'
14   in every way. Help me show others how to use this gift.
15   Ignorance is bliss. And everyone wants to be happy.
16   How can you deny me? I'm perfect.
17
18
19
20
21
22
23
24
25
26
27
28
29
30
31
32
33
34
35

Mr. Rogers and the Bunny Rabbit
by Lynn Roaten Terrell

1 Mr. Rogers — age unspecified   Male/Female

2

3 *(Mr. Rogers, an amusing rascal and mischievous trickster, may*

4 *not be the typical grade school teacher of innocent and*

5 *unsuspecting children. His laughable actions and antics are sure*

6 *to inspire mayhem in any classroom! There is a touch of lunacy*

7 *in the "story time period" as Mr. Rogers percolates with flavorful*

8 *tidbits of gossip in his chronicle of the latest neighborhood news.)*

9

10 Hi, boys and girls. Remember Mr. Kruger, who lives next

11 door? We fed his bunnies while he was on vacation. Well,

12 the very next day, that big old doggy, Festis, surprised

13 Mr. Rogers when he came to the door with one of Mr.

14 Kruger's little baby bunnies in his mouth — his poor

15 little bunny body, badly bruised and covered with brush.

16 Yes, Mr. Bunny Rabbit was just as dead as Old Man

17 Humphrey. So, I scolded the doggy, and told him he was

18 a BAD BOY! Then I shampooed the tiny little body, blow

19 dried its hair, put a pretty pink ribbon on it and placed

20 it — ever so gently — back into its cage. Well, the day

21 the Krugers returned, I saw a big red ambulance cart off

22 poor Mr. Kruger. Mrs. Kruger said, "One of our bunnies

23 died the day before we left, and Mr. Kruger had buried

24 him in the garden. We got in late last night. And this

25 morning, I found Mr. Kruger collapsed beside the bunny

26 hutch. Apparently some MANIACAL FIEND dug up our

27 dead bunny baby, gave him an herbal shampoo, dolled

28 him up with a cute little pink bow — AND PUT HIM

29 BACK IN HIS CAGE for poor, unsuspecting Mr. Kruger

to find!" Well, boys and girls, tomorrow we are going to visit Mr. Kruger in the hospital. We'll take him a nice little stuffed toy. No, NOT a bunny rabbit! Can you say, "Psychiatrist"?

Eden Creek
by Dwight Watson

1 Della — twenty-four   Female
2
3   *(Della, who left a small rural home as a young girl, is now*
4   *twenty-four years old and has returned home after her*
5   *mother's death. In the farmhouse attic, she is busy folding*
6   *and packing old clothes and discarded dishes. Humming as*
7   *she works, Della recalls an incident in her youth that kept her*
8   *isolated from the world. Her haunting "secret" is a human cry*
9   *for compassion and understanding.)*
10
11   *(Loudly)* **Sadie! Did you finish the beans?** *(Slight pause)*
12   **You'd better hurry. Papa will be back soon and, if we**
13   **don't have jars on the boil, he'll wonder what we've**
14   **been doing.** *(She listens)* **I know. I remember. I vowed**
15   **that when I left here I would never snap another bean. I**
16   **swore I would eat grass first. You were too young to**
17   **remember, but each year Mama and I put up to three**
18   **hundred quarts. I washed, snapped, and canned so**
19   **many of those green things I felt, sometimes, if I saw**
20   **one more I would turn green and snap. Mama would**
21   **always stop my complaining by telling me we were lucky**
22   **to have food. 'Poor people have poor ways,' she would**
23   **say. And, 'Eden Creek is full of starving people, sinking**
24   **in the Depression.'** *(Softly)* **Mama was always the star**
25   **performer around here.** *(She folds and packs clothes into*
26   *an empty box.)* **She was proud of the fact that she could**
27   **send Papa to the fields each morning with a full**
28   **stomach. And then she buzzed through the house**
29   **cooking, cleaning, churning, canning, and changing dirty**

1   diapers, and still she caught up with Papa in the field by
2   early afternoon.
3   I even remember seeing Mama stopping at the end
4   of almost every row to nurse you. *(Slightly louder)* That's
5   right, Sadie, you were weaned on snapbeans. We all
6   were. Compared to endless housework, fieldwork
7   must've seemed like a holiday to her. *(She picks up a*
8   *cracked blue pitcher.)* Mama always enjoyed her hands in
9   the soil. Making things grow. Flowers. She loved
10   flowers. *(An imaginary Sadie enters.)* Ahhh! You startled
11   me. When did you sneak up? *(Slight pause)* Are the
12   beans boiling? Good. That should keep Papa happy.
13   Why don't you go through the box over there. I'm
14   making a pile here of things to give or throw away.
15   *(Pause)* No. I think I'll keep the pitcher. *(Pause)* Yes, I
16   know it's cracked, but I'd like to keep it. *(Della places the*
17   *pitcher down in front of her.)*
18   Sadie, Joe is picking me up tomorrow. I'll be going
19   back to Mooresville. I have to be in the factory at eight
20   on Tuesday morning. *(Slight pause)* Yes. I do. It's good
21   work. I really like it, Sadie. I'm making my own way. Joe
22   wants me to marry him, but that means keeping house
23   and having babies. I couldn't do that, not now anyway.
24   And I know Papa wants me to stay here, but I'm lucky
25   to have a job. Maybe I'm selfish, but for the first time I
26   feel like I'm accomplishing something. I can't be like
27   Mama who rushed through household chores so that
28   she could spend a few hours in the field. *(Pause)* Sadie,
29   I'm not that far away. Why don't you plan to spend some
30   time with me. I'll talk to Papa and insist that a girl your
31   age needs to be with her older sister, regularly,
32   especially, now since Mama is gone. I'll tell him there
33   are things we need to share. To discuss. Things you
34   need to know. Things neither he nor his sons can tell
35   you. *(Pause)* What is that? *(Della picks up a shoe box.)* Let

1   me see. *(Embarrassed laugh)* **Oh, me. Sadie, this was my**
2   **curly hair. Yes, curly hair. Not all of us are blessed with**
3   **natural curls, so I invented my own. I was your age,**
4   **twelve, when Papa built the barn. Near his stack of**
5   **lumber, by his sawhorse, was a pile of curly wood**
6   **shavings. I took the longest curls and kept them in this**
7   **box. Occasionally, I'd take them out and bobby pin the**
8   **shavings to my hair, pretending they were ringlets. Like**
9   **this, see?** *(She puts shavings in her hair.)*
10   **I felt beautiful. The Bible says 'A woman's hair is her**
11   **glory.' Well, these ringlets sure made me feel glorious.**
12   *(Slight laugh)* **I was behind the barn one day wearing my**
13   **ringlets when I heard people laughing. I turned and it**
14   **was Papa and our brothers. They had caught me**
15   **pretending with wood shavings in my hair. They began to**
16   **make jokes and laugh. Louder and ... I became**
17   **embarrassed.** *(Quickly)* **And, I don't know why, but I**
18   **began to cry. I ran to the house screaming for Mama.**
19   **'Make them stop! Please, make them stop! Mama!'**
20   *(Thoughtful)* **But Mama could be cold and quiet. She**
21   **said, 'What I had done was silly, and of course people**
22   **were going to laugh.' She made me sit at the table. She**
23   **never stopped cleaning or cooking to even look at me.**
24   **She was carrying you at the time, but no one would know**
25   **it by the way she worked. Besides, she seemed pregnant**
26   **for as long as I can remember. Always round like she**
27   **was going to pop at any moment. I remember yelling at**
28   **Mama, 'Why don't you listen to me? I pushed away from**
29   **the table, and Mama's blue pitcher fell to the floor.**
30   *(Pause. She stares at the pitcher.)*
31   **It didn't shatter, but it did crack. I knew how much**
32   **she loved the blue pitcher. Probably the only piece of**
33   **kitchenware she cared about. I ran to the bedroom,**
34   **crying. A few minutes later she came to me. I thought**
35   **she'd be mad, but she wasn't. She sat beside me and**

1 gently removed the shavings from my hair. 'Della,' she
2 said, 'there's something you will soon learn. There's life
3 in my body, and soon your body is going to change as
4 well. You won't be my little girl any more.' *(She removes*
5 *the shavings from her hair, dropping them into the pitcher.)*
6 She said she couldn't explain exactly but that I would
7 know it when the time came. I was twelve, like you,
8 Sadie. I didn't know what Mama was talking about. *(She*
9 *rises)* Would you have known, Sadie? *(She moves to a*
10 *stack of linen and blankets. Pause)*
11 Two nights later Papa sent me and our brothers to
12 bed early. He said that in the morning there would be a
13 new child in the house. *(Thoughtfully)* I was so afraid.
14 The boys went fast to sleep, but I stayed awake in my
15 bed listening to dogs barking in the distance. Late in the
16 night Mama began to moan and ... my ... body began to
17 ache. *(Quickly)* I heard Papa start the car and drive
18 away. Mama's moans turned into cries and became
19 louder and louder. And with each of her screams, I felt
20 sharp pains shooting through me. I reached under my
21 covers and felt my legs. They were wet. My legs were
22 wet. My white sheets ... wet ... stained with black and
23 red. I was terrified. This is what Mama meant! She
24 meant that I was having a baby! I tried to scream like
25 my Mama, but I was so scared I couldn't make a sound.
26 I felt ... so ... ashamed. So afraid my brothers would
27 wake up and laugh at me for having this baby. *(Slight*
28 *pause)* Later, Mama's cries stopped. Sweating and
29 shaking, I got out of bed. *(She returns to the wooden*
30 *chest.)*
31 I sneaked into Mama's room, and there you were,
32 Sadie, nestled beside Mama. I slipped into bed and
33 snuggled on Mama's other side. We three lay quietly for
34 a long time. Mama stroked my hair. Finally, she said
35 that she needed some rest and she sent me back to my

1   room to sleep. By that time, Papa entered the house with
2   the doctor. I took my bed covers and hid them under my
3   bed. *(Pause)* Early the next morning I slipped out of the
4   house with my sheets. I secretly took them to Eden
5   Creek and washed away the stains as best I could. No
6   one knew I was gone. I held my breath, and was tiptoeing
7   back to my room when I heard Mama calling my name:
8   'Della, here's your new sister. Her name is Sadie.' She
9   handed you to me. *(She crosses behind the stage left chair,*
10   *bends to her knees, holding the chair where the imaginary*
11   *Sadie sits.)*

12   And I held tight to you like you were my own. As I
13   rocked you, I remember telling Mama how sorry I was for
14   breaking her blue pitcher. She said, 'I shouldn't be so
15   sorry. There's nothing we can do about the pitcher now.
16   The important thing today is that Sadie is a healthy
17   baby.' *(She rises and returns to the pitcher.)* Mama didn't
18   throw away the cracked pitcher. Each Sunday, she put it
19   on the kitchen table. She called it her Sunday vase and
20   kept it filled with wild flowers. Every Sunday, Papa
21   wanted to know how the pitcher came to be broken.
22   Mama would smile at me. You see, the two of us shared
23   a very special secret.

24
25
26
27
28
29
30
31
32
33
34
35

Heads
by Jon Jory

1	Rose — age unspecified

Female

2

3 *(Rose, an independent and self-confident woman, has an*
4 *unbridled spirit when it comes to men. She is adventurous*
5 *and cunning, and offers a clinical look at the opposite sex.*
6 *Here, Rose pleads with the women assembled to bid farewell*
7 *to romantic notions of love and marriage. She offers, instead,*
8 *a more realistic game plan to capture an unlikely romance.)*

9

10 Don't kid me, ladies. We are born in America. We are
11 middle-class down to our anklets and add-a-beads. We
12 started learning this stuff with our Barbie dolls. And
13 don't give me any 'traditional roles' stuff. You think guys
14 wouldn't do this if you had these bucks? And if you
15 don't do it, somebody else will. They will line up from
16 here to Nome, Alaska. And what is your responsibility
17 to yourself? Our responsibility is to our potential. Fifty
18 percent of all American marriages end up in divorce
19 anyway and you know what is given as the chief cause?
20 Financial problems. No kidding. Are you doing him a
21 disservice? He's pining away out there. He sits with his
22 back to the cafeteria wall drinking black coffee and
23 wishing he wasn't alone. I mean you aren't hardened
24 cases or something. You can't tell a book by its cover
25 and all that. He's bright. He's a gentleman. Joanie says
26 he practically threw himself over the puddles so she
27 wouldn't get wet. I grant you he's short, shy and
28 myopic, but listen, he is a man among men. What he
29 can do for you, Superman can't do. And, by way of

1   comparison, how hot is anything else we've gotten mixed
2   up with? Your fiance, Margaret, how many dawns and
3   Bloody Marys have we shared while you agonized? I will,
4   I won't, I will, I can't, I love him, I don't, we don't have
5   the same interests, he's cute. Come on, face it. Prince
6   Charles hasn't showed up.
7
8
9
10
11
12
13
14
15
16
17
18
19
20
21
22
23
24
25
26
27
28
29
30
31
32
33
34
35

Snitch

by George K. Cybulski and W. Colin McKay

1 Jerry — age unspecified   Male
2
3   *(Jerry, a small-time petty thief who dreams of big-time*
4   *schemes, lives in a barren underworld of deception and lies.*
5   *He speaks in simple language and provides a candid glimpse*
6   *of a parasite whose hope of an honest, respectable life has*
7   *evaporated. Now, Jerry pleads with a fellow rowdy to join*
8   *him in planning an escapade that promises a new beginning*
9   *in life for both of them.)*
10
11 You ever been in a situation like ... uh ... like ...
12 *(Suddenly inspired)* ... like you are in this little boat, see.
13 An', uh, you're way out in like an ocean or something
14 and ... and your boat's got a leak in it and you're sinkin',
15 see, and, uh, you got nothin' to fix it with and there's
16 sharks all around an' ... an' YA CAN'T SWIM! You know
17 what I mean? You ever been in that kind of situation?
18 Well, that's the way it is with me. I need a new boat. I
19 got some stuff to unload and I need a new boat. *(Sees*
20 *Shakley doesn't get it.)* You remember Eddie Sotello? He
21 got busted the other day. An', he's been fencing some
22 stuff for me. And he's not gonna get out for a long time,
23 so I ... uh ... I need somebody to handle the
24 merchandise for me. *(Sees Shakley still doesn't get it.)*
25 Just forget it, man! Look, there's been these robberies,
26 okay? Jewelry stores. And I'm the runner between the
27 robbers and the fence. Ya follow me so far now? Except
28 now my fence is in County and I'm sittin' on a pile of
29 stuff an' I got no way to move it. They won't know about

1   you. All's they care about's their percentage. I'll tell you
2   where to drop the money and what you gotta do. It's
3   easy. They'll never see you ... you won't see them. And
4   that will give me and Cindy a chance to get the hell outta
5   town before they rip-off another store. Jesus, Shakley!
6   It's the only way I'm gonna get outta this situation.
7   Okay. I gotta leave town. So you'll do it?
8
9
10
11
12
13
14
15
16
17
18
19
20
21
22
23
24
25
26
27
28
29
30
31
32
33
34
35

One Hundred Women
by Kristina Halvorson

1 Nina — young adult   Female
2
3 *(Nina, an agile woman of seductive grace, celebrates her*
4 *emerging womanhood with a sense of courage and quiet*
5 *dignity. Her indomitable spirit is mirrored in the emotional*
6 *turmoil and mental anguish of the "one hundred women"*
7 *that live inside her. The inner strength Nina discovers,*
8 *however, is almost spiritual in its capacity to define her own*
9 *honesty and truthfulness.)*
10
11 There is a place, inside me, where one hundred women
12 live. It is full of light and anything but lonely. I keep Kelly
13 there, and my mother, and my third-grade teacher, Mrs.
14 Rhodes, and my best friend, Christine, from eighth
15 grade, and all the other women who have touched me
16 somehow. There are so many. I close my eyes and I
17 imagine them sitting close together in interlocked
18 circles, talking, holding each other, laughing. Inside me,
19 they know one another. Perhaps some of them are the
20 same. When I am alone I laugh along with them, wrap
21 my arms tight around my breasts, hugging myself,
22 drawing them closer to me. It's only when the men invite
23 themselves in — into the room, into the laughter, even
24 into me — that the links of this, this woman chain are
25 weakened. The men call, and the women come. The
26 circles break apart. I begin to feel like I am coming
27 apart, that my parts are loose and dangling. I hug
28 myself even tighter and rename, reimagine my women.
29 There is at least one hundred of me, without them, I

1　think — Nina the scholar, Nina the poet, the student,
2　the counselor, the lover. I wait for the strongest one of
3　me to step forward so that I can find the right words,
4　summon up the elusive courage to bring back the women
5　I've somehow lost.
6　　And yet, despite my frantic attempts to call forth the
7　philosopher, the diplomat, the encouraging friend,
8　somehow it is always Nina the lover who wins out. She
9　gives into the romance, releases the women to their
10　princes and saviors. Her mother remarries, her
11　schoolteacher moves away with her husband, her best
12　friend falls head over heels for a ninth grader. And Nina
13　the lover nods; Nina the lover knows. She lowers her
14　head and waits for her turn to come, and in the
15　meantime the women fall away from her one by one by
16　one by one ...
17　　What can I do but embrace her, this lover who lives
18　inside my chest; and bid farewell to the other ninety-nine
19　of me, who always retreat in silence. How difficult can it
20　be to call out the name of a friend you're terrified of
21　losing?
22
23
24
25
26
27
28
29
30
31
32
33
34
35

"Bounty," from *Prodigal Kiss*
by Caridad Svich

1   Coral — elderly   Female
2
3   *(Coral, an elderly woman with a youthful look, sits alone on*
4   *a train. She is elegant and sophisticated in her satin-and-lace*
5   *dress and long pearls. Around her neck hangs a small velvet*
6   *bag. The worldly Coral casts a piercing eye on human nature*
7   *and recalls her own humble youth. She exhibits the social*
8   *grace and lovely form of a woman who has discovered the*
9   *secret of personal freedom and liberty.)*
10
11   Nineteen hundred and twenty-nine.
12   That's when I came here from Santiago in Chile.
13   It was another kind of land then.
14   The fields gave you a sense of peace.
15
16   I was a spit of five.
17   Straight off the boat to New York,
18   and the stink of cabbage and fresh fruit.
19   And in the air a sorrowful blues.
20   There was a woman named Bessie who walked down
21   my street
22   with a rope of pearls 'round her neck
23   and the finest feathers in her hair:
24   coq rouge, marabou, and ostrich.
25   She had a voice like thunder.
26   She's say, 'My name is Miss Smith
27   and don't you dare forget it.'
28   She was strange. So different from the women in Chile.
29   And she carried herself in such a way

1	as to say, 'It does not matter what anyone thinks
2	of me.
3	I do as I please.'
4	
5	Here I was. A girl of five. Come all the way from
6	Santiago.
7	Didn't know a thing. Could hardly say my name.
8	
9	
10	
11	
12	
13	
14	
15	
16	
17	
18	
19	
20	
21	
22	
23	
24	
25	
26	
27	
28	
29	
30	
31	
32	
33	
34	
35	

Spirit Awakening
by Akuyoe Graham

1 Unspecified — young adult   Female
2
3   *(A young African woman, who was brought to the United*
4   *States as a girl by her mother, explores her self-identity. In*
5   *highly poetic style, the woman offers a candid view of her*
6   *own life. She recalls her grim childhood, pays tribute to her*
7   *African heritage and sings a jubilant song of the freedom she*
8   *has found in returning to her roots as a spiritual being of*
9   *African descent.)*
10
11   **Woman**
12   **black**
13   **so called weaker sex**
14   **conceived in rivalry**
15   **learned language of the opposition**
16   **gave up my own**
17   **chilling cold**
18   **mamma working long hard hours**
19   **in the house we lived**
20   **a tension-filled house shared with friends**
21   **where the drunken stench and roar of the alcoholic**
22   **neighbor terrified his own and mine into a**
23   **graceless state of jaw-grinding silence**
24   **I was eight**
25   **caroline mensah was dead**
26   **it was night**
27   **the grown ups had gone to mourn**
28   **I was alone in my room**
29   **I was afraid**

1	mr. cunningham was only days dead
2	kofi was a close family friend
3	he was twenty-seven
4	he was a man
5	he was to comfort and protect me
6	I was a child
7	I was eight
8	infant strength
9	trust abused
10	his comfort an act of perversion
11	I closed my eyes
12	feigned sleep
13	held my breath
14	tears caressed my face
15	screams strangled my throat
16	his fingers
17	cold
18	probing
19	their carnal deed to do
20	my stubborn thighs a closed highway
21	his attempted rape
22	my shame
23	my rage and secret pain
24	inability to stand up for myself
25	unspoken
26	finally spoken
27	nineteen years
28	breathing
29	talking
30	understanding myself
31	
32	Free
33	the beautiful ones are yet born
34	they disguise themselves and then the angels can't
35	recognize

1   them anymore
2   mama
3   what lessons and challenges have you buried deep
4   in your
5   womb?
6   endurance isn't always strength
7   yielding too has its place and beauty
8   let's share you and I
9   a help one to another
10   ending this reign of victimhood
11   I see now that I judged you cruelly
12   the pain I feel
13   not being enough
14   you too have been feeling for years
15   your spirit hungering for empowerment
16   how were you to know this would lead
17   you to a barren land where friendships were a luxury
18   and your ebony skin a branding worse than the scarlet
19   letter
20   you had to play your highlife and wear your bright colors
21   to keep a sense of who you were
22   papa
23   when I gave my blessed name did I also give up the
24   part
25   of you in me?
26   all your silence
27   perhaps you've been trying to talk to me
28   perhaps in your silence you were trying to tell me
29   secrets
30   a scornful mother that neglected you
31   a starched father that stifled you
32   sights and sounds of colonial rule which stilled your
33   tongue
34   and made your heart fearful
35   papa I'm listening

1	hum like the wind, pitter patter like the rain
2	roar like a mama lion
3	island in the sun is this the face of the motherland
4	you wanted to
5	see?
6	me and my 'good' hair are moving on
7	giles you've been playing a part I allowed you to play
8	I want to breathe like a feather
9	dream rainbows
10	greet the sun
11	
12	Boldness fill me with your cool purple hues and long
13	legged
14	strides
15	take my spirit upon your wings and let's fly over
16	carmine sunsets
17	as we glide through symphonic waves
18	maybe we'll land in china for a glimpse of that last
19	emperor
20	or on a tahitian island where I'll borne brando's
21	tenth child
22	it's in my blood
23	my father had sixteen
24	we'll have no worries boldness and I
25	we're giving our lives over to Highest Creative Force
26	and in that surrender depositing all worry and fear
27	for an
28	awesome, brow-raising, eye-popping, mouth-dropping
29	moment-to-moment livingness
30	the saboteur's spell broken
31	I'll no longer delay my life with my chronic lateness
32	and upon arrival compare and tell myself that I'm not
33	'good enough'
34	reclaiming a child-like appetite for the spontaneous
35	and simple

1	I am
2	Papa
3	we are
4	i'd forgotten but now I see
5	I am
6	mama
7	we are
8	i'd forgotten but now I see
9	I am
10	mama
11	we are
12	born in the image of mother africa
13	desecrated this beauty
14	with a mask of illusion
15	glory be
16	Ataa — Na Nyonmo
17	mi da boshi
18	Father Mother God
19	I thank you
20	drums talk that talk
21	let the hallelujah chorus sound
22	for now unto forever more
23	I am
24	
25	
26	
27	
28	
29	
30	
31	
32	
33	
34	
35	

New York Trucker
by Alison Rosenfeld-Desmarais

1	Unspecified — adult	Male/Female

2

3 *(This memorable audition script features a strong-armed,*
4 *strong-willed New York truck driver with incredible*
5 *determination and desire! His loss of self-control can't be*
6 *easily dismissed, even though there is a dark comic tone to*
7 *his actions. The incident of road rage he experiences is*
8 *intense and irrational, and his sudden explosion is a*
9 *surprising climax that is sure to shock.)*

10

11 So, you know what de traffic is like on de L.I.E. on a
12 Friday, you know? I mean, jeez. And you know, I'm
13 under like a lotta pressure at my career. All dose
14 packages dat gotta be dere overnight — I'm responsible
15 for a lotta stuff. So I'm drivin' along in my truck nd this
16 jerk comes right along side me in one of dem little
17 sports cars and he's like tryin' to kind of nose me outta
18 de way. And, of course, I'm only worried about dem
19 packages in de back of da truck. So I start thinkin' —
20 don't I have like the obligation to protect all dat stuff?
21 Like, it could be — I don't know — like maybe
22 government stuff or something — like parts for bombs
23 or somethin' in one of dem boxes back dere. And I start
24 thinkin' — what's more important? Some rich guy tryin'
25 to get to his beach house fer the weekend? Or dose
26 maybe very important boxes in de truck ...
27   So I shot him.

28

29

Eating Out
by Marcia Dixcy

1　Pat — late twenties　　　　　　　　　　　　　　　Female

2

3　*(Pat, a thin "All-American" young woman in her late*
4　*twenties, sits quietly at a small table center stage. She*
5　*pauses, looks around cautiously, lights a cigarette and then*
6　*speaks directly to the audience. Pat has an eating disorder*
7　*and her two best friends, Chris and Melanie, are anorexic and*
8　*bulimic. Her descriptive narrative reveals the haunting secrets*
9　*of ritual addiction and drug dependency.)*

10

11　I've tried it all: fasting, puking, laxatives, jogging,
12　aerobics; it's a full-time job. I suppose the next thing will
13　be plastic surgery, liposuction. From what I've read that'll
14　be the wave of the future. And I remember my
15　grandmother telling me that her mother seriously
16　considered having her two lowest ribs removed so she
17　could cinch her corset in tighter. Apparently, there was
18　really a craze for that. So, some things just don't
19　improve. But there are ways to make it easier. Some you
20　can live with, and — some you can't. And I remember the
21　best, really the best for me was in capsule form. It's
22　virtually impossible now, but seven or eight years ago you
23　could still manage to get Control II drugs. At that time I
24　had met a medical student and he knew this resident and
25　we worked out a cooperative system. The resident would
26　write me a prescription. You see, they needed me because
27　they said it would be most unusual for these diet pills to
28　be prescribed for a man. Seems strange, since those
29　doctors really thrived on 'em — particularly mixed with

1   alcohol. But Norman, this medical student, and I would
2   drive outside the city — I was in college in Washington,
3   D.C. — and we would find these smallish towns and I
4   would go in and get the drugs: biamphetamines, they
5   were called Black Beauties.
6   The first time I had one was on a Sunday: a
7   biamphetamine brunch. And to this day, I remember
8   that afternoon, the intensity and the power. The power
9   to keep on going — without sleep, without food. We took
10   this marathon bike ride. I don't even like bike-riding,
11   really, 'cause the cars drive me crazy. But on the speed,
12   it felt like I could pedal right off the earth, right off the
13   rim of the horizon. And it was over forty-eight hours
14   before I ate anything. For awhile, I only took one, once a
15   week. I'd get pretty wiped out, depleted for a few days
16   after. I mean, it's like the adrenaline is coursing through
17   your body, probably burning up about twice the calories.
18   And the weight just really dropped off.
19
20
21
22
23
24
25
26
27
28
29
30
31
32
33
34
35

Death Comes to Us All, Mary Agnes
by Christopher Durang

1 Margot — adult	Female

2

3   *(Margot Pommes, one of the tempestuous eccentrics living in*
4   *her family's decaying mansion, suffers from a series of frightful*
5   *dreams that may reveal dark, unexplained household secrets.*
6   *She is subject to spontaneous outbursts and fits of anxiety as*
7   *her emotions rise and fall. Margot now turns reluctantly to her*
8   *father as she shares one of her most recent dreams.)*

9

10   Last night I had that awful dream again ... I don't mean
11   the Joan of Arc dream. This is the one where I'm in the
12   orphanage and I see my mother in a field with my two
13   brothers, canoeing. And rather than feeling angry at her
14   for putting me in the orphanage, I just feel this terrible
15   longing to be accepted by them, by her. And then I find
16   that I'm dressed like a boy and that I've even grown a
17   mustache, and I go out to them to show my mother that
18   I'm a boy and then I notice that I'm still wearing lipstick,
19   and I try to wipe it off but there's so much of it I can't
20   get it off, and I keep wiping it and wiping it, and the
21   three of them just laugh and laugh at me, and then they
22   steer their canoe at me and it comes racing toward me
23   to crush me, and a great big oar from the canoe hits me
24   on top of the head, and then the oar starts to beat me
25   repeatedly, ecstatically. And then I wake up. Trembling.
26   I feel such anger and unhappiness all the time! When
27   you rescued me from the orphanage, I thought I was

1   finally saved and that things would be all right. But they
2   weren't. You don't hate mother. And you don't like me.
3   What am I to do? I've been seeing my psychiatrist for three
4   years now, four times a week, and I don't feel any change.
5   I feel such a prisoner to my past. And I have such a
6   longing for normality. I see people on the street who eat in
7   cafeterias and have families and go to parks and who
8   aren't burdened with this terrible bitterness; and I want to
9   be like them. So much I want to be like them.

10
11
12
13
14
15
16
17
18
19
20
21
22
23
24
25
26
27
28
29
30
31
32
33
34
35

Stepping Out
by Richard Harris

1   Mavis — adult   Female
2
3   *(Mavis, an ex-professional dancer, volunteers to give lessons*
4   *to a group of middle-aged women — and one shy, reclusive*
5   *man — in a local church hall north of London, England. The*
6   *weekly tap dancing class is a series of outrageous mishaps*
7   *and missteps for the aspiring performers, and the self-mocking*
8   *Mavis has quite a task at hand in trying to rehearse this crew*
9   *for a grand charity show performance!)*
10
11 Okay, everyone, let's get on, shall we? It's our first
12 rehearsal, so lots of concentration, yes? *(Indicating)*
13 Rose, Sylvia and Andy — we'll take you three at the
14 back — no, Rose in the middle please. Then we'll have
15 Maxine, Vera, Lynne and Dorothy — spread yourselves
16 out so you can be seen. But come forward a step, you're
17 crowding — and Geoffrey, let's have you at the front,
18 directly in front of Rose.
19   Okay. So you're standing with your backs to the
20 audience ... *(She will demonstrate, turning her back to*
21 *them.)* Feet apart, and absolutely perfectly still —
22 nothing moving. The curtains or the lights come up or
23 whatever and you stay there, not moving, absolutely
24 static still. For four counts you do absolutely nothing.
25   On given counts, back line, middle line and Geoffrey
26 turn around and face the front. No, you don't move your
27 feet and so your legs are crossed ... From there you
28 bring the right arm up, leaving the left arm down, you
29 lift the hat and you hold it high — yes? On counts three

1   and four, line of four does exactly the same thing but
2   when you turn you leave the right arm down, holding the
3   hat low. Incidentally, there's going to be some fast
4   bouncing around and you might have bust troubles, so
5   wear something good and firm, yes? *(Generally)* Right.
6   We'll have the first four bars and make sure the intro is
7   spot on — it's got to be good, it's got to have panache,
8   it's got to have the three T's. What are the three T's?
9   Tits, teeth and tonsils.

10   *(Demonstrates)* You smile, you stick your chest out,
11   you look like you're enjoying it. You've only got two T's,
12   haven't you, Geoffrey? Okay, let's have you in your
13   opening positions and we'll try it again. Quick as you
14   can, please Rose, we've got to get through! Dorothy —
15   just a little smaller ... Sylvia, can we get rid of the gum?
16   I want to see your teeth, not hear them! All right? And
17   it's five six seven eight ... Da da da dada da for nothing.
18   Da da da dada da back line ... Da da da dada da middle
19   line ... Sway, sway Geoffrey! Okay. I think the problem is
20   that when you turn, some of you are a little off balance.
21   Right, back into position please and we'll do it again —
22   other way round please, Sylvia — and it's five six seven
23   eight. *(Demonstrates)* Then ... shuffle ball change, shuffle
24   ball change shuffle ball change, six tap springs and hold.
25   Right. Now, let's try it to the music!
26
27
28
29
30
31
32
33
34
35

Amara
by Leigh Podgorski

1   Deiter — twenties   Male

2

3   *(Deiter Olbrych, a young, overly dramatic actor in his*
4   *twenties, confronts the playwright about rewrites for his*
5   *character Johnny Jakes in the script* Dance with Death. *He*
6   *is a brash egotist, unabashedly vain in his exaggerated sense*
7   *of self-importance. Deiter's zeal in playing a blood-and-guts*
8   *fictional stage character may lead us to wonder if his real life*
9   *role is acted out with the same passion.)*

10

11   Eva! Eva! There you are! I've been looking all over for
12   you. Have you got the rewrites? Gwynne told me you
13   were going to change the ending. That now, instead of
14   Johnny slicing Mary open with a knife, he's going to
15   smash her brains out with the fire poker. Oh, God, Eva,
16   that's brilliant. Absolutely brilliant playwriting. I mean,
17   the whole piece is brilliant, of course, what else could it
18   be. I think it's going to make my career, actually, but
19   this latest idea, this is absolutely smashing. What took
20   you so long to come up with it? No, no, I understand. I
21   mean, writing a play. I could never even attempt it. Well,
22   maybe I could. But the fire poker. Wow. That's exactly
23   who Johnny Jakes is. Savage. Wild. Out of control.
24   When Gwynne told me you were going to change the
25   ending, Eva, I was so excited I couldn't sleep. All last
26   night, I tossed and turned, the images just flying at me
27   so fast, I couldn't stop them. I couldn't turn them off.
28   God!
29   What drama! Picture it. The stage, splattered with

1   blood. Me, splattered with blood. I enter for my curtain
2   call, exhausted, spent, covered with blood. I bow. Barely
3   able to move from the exhaustion. The crowd goes wild.
4   Oh, Eva, Johnny has just got to bludgeon Mary to death
5   with that fire poker. Gwynne promised me you would
6   change the ending. I know how these things work. I know
7   the theatre. I know drama. You give me a character, any
8   character, and I'll make him fly. I've proved it with
9   Johnny Jakes, haven't I? Oh, I'd make a devastating
10   playwright, if I could ever find the time to just sit down
11   and do it. Eva, I know who Johnny Jakes is. I know how
12   he thinks. I know what he feels. Christ, Eva, I know what
13   the guy eats for breakfast. He has got to smash Mary's
14   brains out with that fire poker. That's the only way the
15   play will work. That's the only way Johnny Jakes would
16   kill.
17
18
19
20
21
22
23
24
25
26
27
28
29
30
31
32
33
34
35

A Woman Called Truth
by Sandra Fenichel Asher

1   Sojourner Truth — adult   Female

2

3   *(Sojourner Truth, the African American historical figure who was*

4   *active in the abolition of slavery and women's rights movements,*

5   *provides an inspiring chronicle of individual courage and*

6   *indomitable spirit in this authentic character portrait. Although a*

7   *monumental force in shattering the chains of slavery, "Truth" is*

8   *also a flesh-and-blood woman with a warm sense of humor.)*

9

10 *(Resuming narrative)* **I began walking east again, as I'd**

11 **walked before toward freedom. Though I could neither**

12 **read nor write, I could talk and I could sing. I would**

13 **wander the country, talking and singing, until the people**

14 **heard and understood, and made wrong things right. In**

15 **parlors and in lecture halls, on street corners and in revival**

16 **tents, I told my story — as I'm telling it to you — to any**

17 **and all with a moment to listen. I spoke out against**

18 **slavery and poverty and ignorance. I cried out for justice.**

19 **'Sojourner,' I became, a wanderer among the**

20 **people. 'Lord,' I cried, 'Thy name is truth,' and I took for**

21 **my own name the name of my last and greatest and only**

22 **master. My name, my free name, my own name:**

23 **Sojourner Truth.** *(She speaks from lectern as if addressing*

24 *a public gathering. Others ad-lib responses as at opening.)*

25 **Children, I have come here tonight like the rest of you,**

26 **to hear what I have got to say.** *(She laughs at her own*

27 *joke.)* **Children, I talk to God, and God talks to me. I go**

28 **out and talk to God in the fields and the woods. This**

29 **morning I was walking out, and I got over the fence. I**

saw the wheat holding up its head, looking very big. I
went up and took hold of it. You believe it? There was no
wheat there! I said, 'God, what is the matter with this
wheat?' And He says to me, 'Sojourner, there's a little
weevil in it.' Now, I hear talk about the Constitution and
the rights of man. I come up and I take hold of this
Constitution. It looks mighty big and I feel for my rights,
but there aren't any there. Then I say, 'God, what ails
this Constitution?' And He says to me, 'Sojourner,
there's a little weevil in it.' Well, now, don't these little
weevils just eat up this country's crop? *(Others applaud.*
She steps to side of lectern.)

    In my travels, I met Frederick Douglass, fighting for
the black people, and Susan B. Anthony, fighting for the
woman's right to vote. Harriet Beecher Stowe, Ulysses
S. Grant. *(She takes a small book from her pocket and*
shows it.) Got all their autographs right here. I call this
my Book of Life. *(She opens book and runs her fingers over*
a signature, reciting rather than reading.) Says, 'October 29,
1864,' doesn't it? 'A. Lincoln.' *(She smiles affectionately at*
the page.) Shook his hand at the White House. Yes, I did.
I said, 'Mr. Lincoln, I never heard of you before you ran
for president.' He said, 'Sojourner, I have heard of you.'
(She pauses, saddened.) Saw him one last time ... to say
goodbye. Rest well, Father Abraham. So much done; so
much left to do. *(She returns to the cube RD of the podium,*
where she sits as at the opening of the play. Others take their
places for final scenes as if gathering for a public hearing.)

    It was with Frances Gage at a women's rights
convention in Ohio that I gave one special talk of mine.
Some folks liked it; plenty didn't. But everybody listened,
and they all remembered.

Happy Birthday, Dad
by Don P. Norman

1   Steve — twenty-one   Male

2

3   *(Steve Manning, twenty-one-year-old son of a local politician,*

4   *is the only survivor of a group of young people who were*

5   *beaten, sexually assaulted, and then murdered while on a*

6   *camping trip. When complete details of what actually took*

7   *place were left unanswered, Steve's father invented a story*

8   *cooked up by his own publicist that made his son a local hero.*

9   *Now, Steve confronts his estranged father about the incident.)*

10

11   We weren't telling you everything for a reason, to spare

12   some good people more agony. So, you want the truth,

13   huh? Well, here it is. They killed Rick and the girls, Dad,

14   and they did rob us first. But it never occurred to you that

15   when they raped Christine and Patti and Susan, that

16   maybe they didn't stop there. That's right, Father — they

17   robbed and raped US. ALL OF US. And I am not standing

18   here today because I'm some kind of ... tough guy. Rick

19   is dead and I'm still alive because I was a coward.

20   I didn't black out like I said before. I saw everything.

21   I had just come back from taking a leak, and I

22   remember looking at my watch and seeing it was about

23   two-thirty. It was maybe a minute after I got back into

24   my sleeping bag, that I heard a scream. It sounded like

25   Patti. I was trying to get up, and somebody hit me. A

26   couple of times. I don't know what they hit me with, a

27   gun, maybe. I was dizzy, and they dragged me out of the

28   tent. I don't know how many there were: six, seven,

29   maybe more. I heard a struggle behind me, and I knew

1   Rick was out there, too, and they had him. I tried to get
2   up even though they were holding me down, and
3   somebody hit me again, and I remember thinking that I
4   wished they would just kill me and get it over with. We
5   could hear the girls screaming far off somewhere, back
6   in the woods, and they were laughing. The bastards were
7   laughing, and then somebody said something about
8   getting in on the fun. They tore off my shorts ...
9   somebody cut them and ripped them off the rest of the
10 way, and I knew what was coming next. Then I felt less
11 hands holding me down, and I heard different screaming.
12 I was able to look up. Rick was there — he was on the
13 back of one of them, and had him in a headlock so he
14 couldn't get him off. That was our chance. I should've
15 done something then. Then another one crept up behind
16 Rick. I saw him pull his head back, and then take his
17 knife ... the blood, the blood splashed on me, on my
18 face, in my mouth ... then ... then they took him down,
19 and I heard him ... I heard the sound of him choking on
20 his own blood, and they still raped him. Dad ... Rick was
21 dying, and they still raped him. Somebody put their foot
22 on my head, and shoved my face into the dirt ... then it
23 was my turn ... there were about four, five of them. I
24 wasn't counting, the agony was there the whole time. I
25 never even felt it, until I ... until I didn't hear Rick
26 anymore ...
27   When it was finally over, I really wanted them to kill
28 me ... I thought, when I heard them whispering together,
29 that they might let me live. Ever been stabbed, Father?
30 It's like being raped all over again, but they're destroying
31 your soul and your body at the same time. They stabbed
32 me four times. I held my breath, and played dead.
33 Somebody kicked me, and I didn't move. It was like
34 swimming in a pool of red water. There was blood and
35 there was pain, and the sound of my heart beating, and

1 I wondered if I would even know when the sound
2 stopped.
3   After forever, they left. I wanted to scream at the
4 pain, but I dragged myself over to Rick. They had gutted
5 him after they finished with him. His eyes were open,
6 and they were staring back at where they'd had me. And
7 I can't help thinking, that the whole time, all he was
8 thinking about was helping me ... while he was dying, all
9 he thought of was me ... That mean anything to you,
10 Dad? Figure it out, yet? Remember before the trip, when
11 I had something to tell you, but you didn't have time? I
12 was too much of a coward to tell you after that. That
13 was the whole reason why Rick and I went on the trip.
14 To figure it out. To decide if we would tell you and Mr.
15 and Mrs. Callaway, and how we would do it. But I was
16 afraid to tell you, and afraid to die. So Rick is dead, and
17 now I've lost my best friend ... and my lover.
18   That's right, Dad. Your big, strapping linebacker son is
19 a flaming faggot. Rick and I have been lovers for the last
20 year, and you and his father, the Great Men of Local
21 Politics, didn't have a clue. And if you had, all you
22 would've cared about would be your precious careers. I
23 think that whoever attacked us, they knew. They knew
24 that I wasn't dead, and that I'd suffer a lot more if they let
25 me live. And they were right. I'm even too much of a
26 coward to kill myself. But right now, if I had to do it all
27 again, I wouldn't hesitate to take Rick's place. And the
28 worst part of it all? Losing my friends? Losing the one
29 person in the world I'll ever love? Coming this close to
30 death? No, Father. The worst thing of all, is that part of
31 me still feels like I deserve what happened because I'm not
32 the son you always wanted me to be, and I never will be.
33   So now you know. Is this what you wanted? You
34 happy, now? By the way, it's after midnight. Happy
35 Birthday, Dad. Happy Birthday.

Two Minutes Too Long
by Colin Donald

1   The multiple voices of four young adults cast a dark,
2   ominous shadow over the competitive games adolescents
3   play. There is a flavor of innocent simplicity in the
4   character portraits, but the script has a serious undertone
5   that calls attention to the surprising climax. Try to imagine
6   the psychological frame of mind at work in the game the
7   characters play. Approach the scene with a juvenile
8   attitude but peer beneath the surface to discover the more
9   competitive, increasingly intense nature of the contest.
10   Exaggerated poses and facial expressions should be
11   avoided and the focus should be on character actions.
12   Although the scene begins as a childish game, it abruptly
13   ends as a cruel joke.
14

15 Macca — young adult   Male
16 Lucy — young adult   Female
17 Dimitri — young adult   Male
18 Craig — young adult   Male
19

20 *(Three young adults — Macca, Lucy, and Dimitri — are*
21 *playing a game in a deserted schoolyard. Dimitri, calmly*
22 *seated in a Lotus position, is in an almost spiritual trance. The*
23 *other young adults surround him in a semi-circle, and Macca*
24 *holds a watch in his hand. There is a sense of urgency in the*
25 *air as each of the characters struggles to make sense of the*
26 *nonsense going on.)*
27

28 **MACCA: Fifteen seconds!**
29 **CRAIG:** *(Enters)* **Hey Macca, what's going on?**

1 MACCA: Quiet, Craig!

2 CRAIG: What?

3 MACCA: Hang on, Dimitri's holding his breath.

4 LUCY: Not for too long I hope.

5 MACCA: Thirty seconds!

6 CRAIG: What's this all about?

7 MACCA: He's got to make two minutes. You are going to
8   make two minutes, aren't you mate? *(DIMITRI*
9   *momentarily breaks out of his calm to smile and nod.)*

10 LUCY: God, I hope not.

11 MACCA: Lucy loses the bet if he does.

12 CRAIG: Cool. What did you bet?

13 LUCY: You'd rather not know.

14 MACCA: Forty-five seconds!

15 LUCY: What was I thinking?

16 CRAIG: Hey, com'on guys, what's the bet?

17 MACCA: Think. What does Dimitri want from Lucy?

18 LUCY: Macca!

19 MACCA: Hey, it wasn't my idea. You cooked your own
20   goose, my dear.

21 CRAIG: Lucy, you didn't! After all this time? Really?

22 MACCA: One minute!

23 LUCY: It's not over yet. There's another minute left. It'll be
24   getting harder for him all the time. I can still win.

25 MACCA: Only if he takes a breath. He's looking pretty good
26   to me, Lucy.

27 LUCY: Craig, help me.

28 CRAIG: What?

29 LUCY: Make him take a breath. Distract him, tell him a
30   joke or something. Please.

31 CRAIG: Are you kidding? It'll be a classic if you lose this
32   bet.

33 MACCA: One minute and fifteen seconds!

34 LUCY: I'll pay you! Twenty bucks.

35 CRAIG: I'm not that cheap. Not for something like this.

1   LUCY: Alright, thirty!

2   CRAIG: Time's running out.

3   LUCY: Forty dollars, that's all I've got!

4   MACCA: One minute and thirty seconds!

5   CRAIG: It's a deal. Hey, Dimitri, your fly is undone. *(DIMITRI*

6   *does not flinch.)*

7   LUCY: That's no good. You've got to do better.

8   CRAIG: Hmmm. OK for forty bucks, here goes. Hey Dimitri,

9   cop an eyeful of this. *(CRAIG drops his pants. DIMITRI just*

10   *smiles and closes his eyes.)*

11 MACCA: One minute and forty-five seconds! Sorry Lucy, I

12   reckon Dimitri's going to collect.

13 LUCY: *(Getting distressed)* Oh, hell. He can't make it. He

14   musn't!

15 CRAIG: Guess it's the end of the road, Lucy.

16 MACCA: Five, four, three, two, one. Two minutes!

17 CRAIG: Yo, Dimitri! What a man. *(LUCY cries. DIMITRI does*

18   *not move.)*

19 MACCA: Hey pal, no showing off. It's time for Lucy's big pay

20   out! *(MACCA touches DIMITRI, who topples over sideways.)*

21 CRAIG: He's dead!

22 LUCY: *(Joyously)* I WON!

23

24

25

26

27

28

29

30

31

32

33

34

35

VOICES OF FANTASY AND FUN

Voices of Fantasy and Fun

The voices of fantasy and fun depict characters living in a topsy-turvy world that has lost its meaning. Sometimes silly or even foolish, characters are in a constant struggle to regain a sense of meaning and self-identity. Their distorted dreams, fantasies, strange behaviors, or nightmares encourage more theatrical performance styles and call attention to the eccentricities of each character portrait. The scripts are clever, imaginative, and original. They offer far-fetched views of the world and poke fun at present day topics or events. There is a biting and stinging edge to some of the character portraits that voice piercing judgments on the world in rather bold language.

In playing these voices you should allow the incongruity between what the dialog "says" and what the character "does" to provoke the laughter. Pay careful attention to gestures and facial expressions to help mirror the interior feelings and thoughts of the characters. There may be opportunities to assume mechanical posture, engage in machine-like movement, or voice gibberish and nonsense phrases. It is important, however, that you appear sensible and believable no matter what the character behavior might happen to be. It is probably a good idea not to "think" too much as you review these scripts — but rely on your comic impulse and improvisation to flesh out memorable character portraits.

Little Red Riding Hood's Mother
by Tammy Ryan

1   Joan — age unspecified   Female

2

3   *(Joan, an eccentric mother, has recently moved to the country*

4   *with her daughter. She is disturbed to learn that young girls in*

5   *the area are being abducted at school bus stops. Here she*

6   *laments the tragic situation and offers a cynical view of a world*

7   *in which such conduct is possible. There is genuine, sudden wit*

8   *in her maternal instinct that captures the hilarity of the moment.)*

9

10   **This is what I want to know: how come we never hear the**

11   **story about Little Red Riding Hood's Mother? What about**

12   **her side of it? Standing on the doorstep, watching Little**

13   **Red as she disappears round the bend into the dark**

14   **woods. Heart beating, hands wringing, hyperventilating,**

15   **completely powerless, frozen on that doorstep? What the**

16   **hell was the matter with her? Letting her defenseless**

17   **child walk through the woods by herself with a maniac**

18   **wolf on the loose? She knew full well that forest was full**

19   **of wolves, but she sent her out there with a basket of**

20   **bait! 'Stay on the path,' like that's gonna save her. It's**

21   **almost like she wanted Little Red out of the way … Maybe**

22   **she couldn't stand the pressure of living in the woods**

23   **anymore, the isolation, doing nothing but baking cookies**

24   **for her sick mother. And you never hear about that**

25   **relationship. Why doesn't she visit her sick mother**

26   **herself? And where was Little Red's father? No one ever**

27   **addresses that. And what about the Woodcutter? A**

28   **strange man in the woods with an ax. Why does everyone**

29   **automatically trust him? It's a frightening story.**

Magenta Shift
by Carol Mack

1   Jane — mid thirties   Female

2

3   *(Jane, a comedic type in her mid thirties, dashes into a subway*

4   *station to flee a mysterious pursuer. She is a photographer and*

5   *multiple cameras hang from her neck. Rushing up to Rhea, the*

6   *subway booth operator, Jane bursts forth with a complicated*

7   *but sharply worded explanation of the "magenta shift" she's*

8   *experiencing. Her puzzling riddles are all left unanswered.)*

9

10   Listen, first I better tell you the problem. I mean the

11   heart of the problem. O.K.? Did you ... did you ever hear

12   of the Magenta Shift? It's what's happening to all our

13   photographs. The problem started with the Kennedy

14   photographs. The color? See when all those

15   photographs aged, the color started to shift. And then

16   the first dominant color was magenta, which is how they

17   named it the Magenta Shift and then ... what happens

18   is there's a slow fade. A fade to absolutely nothing! And

19   that's the problem. Everything's fading out! Soon

20   there'll be no record at all. Of anything! *(Jane sits,*

21   *overwhelmed with that).*

22   That was only the background. I can only tell this a

23   piece at a time. It's too powerful. So ... O.K., about a

24   month ago a woman calls my studio. She says her

25   wedding pictures are turning pink. All the bridesmaids

26   who'd been wearing blue are now wearing magenta.

27   O.K., I say, calm down. Just take them out of your

28   album and put them in the refrigerator. See, she's gotta

29   put them in the refrigerator or else her wedding cake

1   turns magenta, and then slowly the entire party would
2   lose that color and fade out like it never even happened!
3   It's guaranteed to keep in cold storage for more than five
4   hundred years. Five. Hundred. Years! Get it?

5   *(Intensely)* Don't you get it? Five hundred years!
6   Who's gonna look in Mrs. Sugarman's refrigerator?
7   Where is her refrigerator going to BE in five hundred
8   years? That's from Columbus to now! That's from like
9   Decartes to Derrida! At the rate we're going? That
10   refrigerator will be under some lifeless sea. ALL our
11   photographs are turning moon-color as we talk, and who
12   cares? What are photographs but a collection of silver
13   specks! Somebody's got to BE there to decode them!
14   *(Beat)*

15   All those photos are dots. They're all just moments.
16   They have absolutely no meaning without people to
17   experience them! Oh my God! And how about our
18   books? Disintegrating? *(Claps her hands)* Now, this
19   second fifty million words just went. It's tragic in the
20   stacks. And all those bindings! They want to put it all
21   on microfilm, send the books to Greenland and sink
22   them under the ice. Kids will grow up and not know
23   what a page is! What's left? Frozen books? Who's going
24   to defrost them! Who?

25
26
27
28
29
30
31
32
33
34
35

The Interview
by Jill Morley

1   Laura — age unspecified   Female
2

3   *(Laura, an insecure actress with a dark, brooding*
4   *temperament, is being interviewed by a theatre casting*
5   *director. She is a larger-than-life social misfit in the middle of*
6   *an unmistakable personal identity crisis. Laura's lack of self-*
7   *confidence accurately reflects her inability to make*
8   *appropriate choices, and her prospects for a successful*
9   *interview are minimal, to say the least.)*
10

11   **Don't you have a scene for me to read? I am so boring.**
12   **I am not one of these personality actresses. I'm**
13   **completely devoid of personality. You're probably**
14   **looking for one of those fun-loving, festive girls and**
15   **that's not me. You see, I don't wear green on St.**
16   **Patrick's Day. I'm not the kind of girl who dresses for**
17   **the holidays.**
18   **I'm anti-holiday.**
19   **I don't know what it is ... I have friends. They like**
20   **me. I'm not even shy. Just ... When I was in the third**
21   **grade, I wrote an essay for my teacher, Miss Laskowski.**
22   **The theme was, 'I'll Never Forget The Day.'**
23   **I wrote something like, 'I'll never forget the day my**
24   **father brought us ducklings. It was such a surprise. The**
25   **smallest one was Milk. The next smallest was**
26   **Quackers. The biggest was Harold. Milk was the first**
27   **one to die ... '**
28   **I went on to coldly describe how each one of them**
29   **got killed by my dog. I was a dark child.**

1   In the margin, Miss Laskowski wrote, 'I enjoyed your
2 story! Very good.'
3   She probably thought I would grow up to be an axe
4 murderer. But instead, here I am, an actress. *(Laughs*
5 *nervously)*
6   Oh! I started working this receptionist job but I'm
7 terrible! I'm not built to 'receive' people. I can't
8 synthesize a genuine smile to random people, strangers.
9 Who cares? I don't know them and the temp agency
10 certainly isn't paying me the big bucks.
11   Are you sure you don't want me to read something?
12 I really feel uncomfortable ... A scene? A poem? The
13 telephone book? Because even that is going to be more
14 interesting than ... excuse me ... can I do a monologue?
15
16
17
18
19
20
21
22
23
24
25
26
27
28
29
30
31
32
33
34
35

First Time
by Ludmilla Bollow

1 Tracy — teenager   Female

2

3 *(Tracy, an apprehensive teenager, silently enters an upscale*

4 *beauty salon. She stops abruptly, looks in the mirror, and*

5 *then carelessly fondles her hair. Tracy is on an adventurous*

6 *journey, and yet there is an emotional struggle taking place*

7 *as she tries to wrestle with her anxiety. This is a lighthearted,*

8 *sentimental script, and Tracy's unfailing warmth needs to*

9 *emerge in performance.)*

10

11 Hi, I'm Tracy Morgan. I have a 9:30 appointment ... No,

12 I don't know who with — they didn't say, it was so hard

13 to understand all the questions. *(Pause.)* Yes, yes — I

14 want it all cut off. *(Bites lips.)* That's what I said — All of

15 it! But, I don't want it thrown away — I mean I can keep

16 it, can't I? I want — I need to ... I should sit here? Okay.

17 *(Sits in chair.)*

18   You don't have to wash it. I did that already, early,

19 so it wouldn't take so long being here. I want it over and

20 done with, soon as possible. And it takes forever to

21 wash and dry —. But I always enjoyed doing it, as if it

22 were a personal pet of mine, part of me I had to groom,

23 care for each day.

24   *(Looks terrified.)* Those are the scissors you use? I

25 don't know, I just thought they'd be smaller. I know it's

26 not going to hurt, but I feel like, well, like before I go to

27 the dentist, and I always have this dread of everything

28 that 'might hurt.'

29   Can you cover the mirror, please. I don't want to see,

1   not till it's over. Thanks. Eech. I can hear the cutting. I
2   never heard such a sound, almost as if the hair's crying.
3   No, I'm not going to cry, except I didn't know what to
4   expect — I've never had my hair cut — No, never. My
5   hair was my mother's pride and joy. She'd wash it, dry
6   it, sometimes braid it. She said it was my trademark —
7   to never cut it — because I'd lose so much of my
8   personality if I did. Head feels lighter already. You're only
9   half through? No — I don't want to look, not till it's all
10 done. 'Cause then I might tell you to stop, and then I'd
11 end up with only half a head of hair. I'd really look
12 strange then, wouldn't I? *(Pause.)*
13   What made me decide to cut my hair? Well — well —.
14 *(Pause.)*
15   A present. Yes, a present. Okay, you see, my mom,
16 my dear sweet mom, she has cancer, and she had to
17 have her head shaved — from the chemo. So, I thought,
18 they could make a wig, from my hair. She refuses to
19 wear a synthetic one. So this would be real hair, my
20 hair. I think she'd like that, my hair, always close to her.
21   You know a place that makes such wigs — here in
22 town? Great! I don't want to have to wait too long. I
23 don't know how long mom has ... But this hair was
24 taking too much time for me anyway. My mom needs my
25 time now.
26   Do you think it'll make a good wig? I mean, can they
27 style it for an older person? I've been saving my waitress
28 money —. *(Shakes her head about.)* It's done? All cut off
29 now? Okay, you can take the towel off the mirror.
30 *(Pause.)*
31   Oh my god — I'm a whole different person. So grown
32 up. I can't wait to show mom!
33
34
35

Golden Arches
by Jared DeFife

1	Unspecified	Male

2

3 *(An anxious, unnamed figure stands at the service counter of a*
4 *fast food restaurant and waits patiently to place an order. This*
5 *clever audition script relies on a vivid self-image and inventive*
6 *mannerisms to provide a fresh character portrait. The audience*
7 *response may be more of a belly laugh than a wry smile, so*
8 *take some risks in your performance of this very familiar event.)*

9

10 I love McDonald's. I used to hate the place, but after many
11 years of intensive therapy I have overcome my 'issues'
12 with this fine dining establishment. You see, I no longer
13 mind waiting in line for nearly an hour ... even though this
14 is a fast food restaurant. But I understand. I just stand
15 back and wait calmly while the kid at the front of the line
16 begs his mom for a Happy Meal. I don't even care that he's
17 drooling all over the counter where my food is supposed to
18 go! All right, that's it! *(To woman at front of the line)* You! ...
19 get the kid his damn HAPPY Meal! *(To girl behind counter)*
20 You! Get your little preadolescent heiney back there, throw
21 nine of those frozen chicken chunks into that primordial
22 ooze that you call 'grease,' grab me a large fry, and while
23 you are at it *(Climbing on counter)* put a little MORE salt on
24 them so that the massive heart attack can hit me
25 BEFORE I can reach the phone to dial 9-1-1! *(Pause)* No, I
26 will NOT repeat that order ... try learning to use a Q-TIP!
27 *(Pause)* TO-GO! *(Throws money at the girl)* Thank you!
28 *(Takes bag and begins to calm down)* No ... you have a nice
29 day. *(Opens bag)* Hey, I ordered a 9-PIECE!

Disturbed
by Brad Boesen

1   Daphne — young adult   Female

2

3   *(Daphne, an unsuspecting young woman, is seated next to*

4   *Bob in the reception lounge of a large hospital. Bob, meeting*

5   *Daphne for the first time, reveals that his father shot himself*

6   *and that it was he who rushed him to the hospital. After*

7   *Daphne has expressed her sympathy, Bob admits that he*

8   *was only joking! This news is disturbing for Daphne, who*

9   *then offers her own "true confession" in retaliation.)*

10

11   You want to hear a joke about my father? One night,

12   when I was twelve years old, my father decided to

13   decorate the house for Christmas. He'd never done it

14   before, but this year he had just gotten a raise at work,

15   and I guess he wanted to show off to the rest of the

16   neighborhood. So about a week before Christmas, dad

17   went out and bought up all of the lights and decorations

18   he could find. It had all been pretty much picked over by

19   then. There wasn't much left, but he still got a lot. One

20   store owner was so glad to get rid of everything so close

21   to Christmas that he threw in an old mannequin and

22   Santa costume that had been cluttering up his store

23   room. Dad brought it home and built his whole display

24   around it. *(Pause. Smiles at the memory of it.)*

25   We didn't have a big brick chimney like you see in

26   books and movies, so instead of that, he put Santa on

27   the roof of the porch, peering into the window of my

28   parents' bedroom. Around all of the windows, he put red

29   lights. Green lights around the edge of the roof. And

1   combinations of the two all criss-crossed up and down
2   and in all of the bushes and trees. It was beautiful. I
3   remember it was really cold that year, so he did all this
4   with these great big boots and gloves ... a huge coat that
5   he had just bought with the money from his raise. And
6   I couldn't imagine how, with all those heavy clothes on,
7   he could climb up that ladder and hang all those lights,
8   but he did. He hung all of them, and in between each
9   string of lights, he would come down the ladder, pick me
10   up off the ground, spin me around, and sit me up on his
11   shoulders to get a better look.

12   It took almost a week to finish it, to get it just the
13   way he wanted it, but when he finally lit it all up, the
14   whole town came out to see it. Everyone! Cars driving
15   around the block over and over again to look at our
16   house. I was so happy. I was sure that this was going to
17   be the best Christmas in the history of Christmases;
18   living in this ... cocoon of color and light, with the rest of
19   the world lining up outside to admire it. On Christmas
20   Eve, dad went downtown to this bar that he used to hang
21   out in. He liked to spend Christmas Eve with his buddies
22   because, on Christmas, all the aunts and uncles would
23   be over, and I guess being hung-over gave him an excuse
24   not to be a good host. *(Small pause)*

25   So, anyway, by the time he got home, it was way
26   past midnight, mom and I were in bed, and mom had
27   turned out all the Christmas lights for the night — she
28   couldn't sleep when they were on, because they would
29   shine in through her window — so the only light was
30   from the street light at the end of the block, and I guess,
31   in the darkness, after drinking all night, dad forgot about
32   the Santa mannequin ... mistook it for a burglar or
33   something because I woke up to hear shouting out on
34   the lawn ... gunshots ... breaking glass. I ran into mom
35   and dad's room, because I didn't know what was

1   happening, but mom and dad weren't in bed. And it
2   was cold, like someone had left the window open, so I
3   looked ... and there was my mother, just lying there on
4   the floor, in the middle of all this shattered glass and
5   blood. She must have been standing at the window
6   when ... *(Pause. Bob is now frozen. Daphne is staring into*
7   *space — reliving the story as she tells it.)*
8   And I just stood there ... I couldn't move. I couldn't
9   say anything. I was still half asleep. It was like a dream.
10   But then I heard the front door open, and footsteps
11   running up the stairs. I was terrified. I thought that
12   whoever had been shouting out on the lawn must be
13   coming to get me now, and I couldn't hide. There was
14   no place to hide. And the only thing I could think of to
15   do was lay down beside my mother and play dead. I
16   thought whoever it was wouldn't hurt me if they thought
17   I was already dead. So, when dad got to the door of the
18   bedroom, he saw me and my mother and all that blood,
19   and ... he said ... something ... it didn't register at first,
20   I was so scared, and concentrating so hard on not
21   moving ... and then he stumbled backwards out of the
22   room, and I heard him crying and saying, 'No, no, no' ...
23   over and over again ... 'No, no, no' ... *(Pause)* and I
24   recognized his voice. I realized it was dad. But before I
25   could say anything there was another gunshot. *(Pause)*
26   And then he wasn't crying anymore. *(Pause)*
27   [Bob]: God ...
28   I guess he didn't have time to leave a funny note like
29   your dad.
30
31
32
33
34
35

The Baptist Gourmet
by Jill Morley

1   Tulula — adult   Female

2

3   *(Tulula, an eccentric Southern belle and a galloping gourmet*

4   *in the kitchen, has her own weekly cable cooking show. She*

5   *dispenses tasty culinary secrets and juicy tidbits of gossip*

6   *like salt and pepper to whet the taste of the small town wives*

7   *who watch her show to relieve their own boredom. In this*

8   *week's show, Tulula shares a recipe that was, by her own*

9   *account, divinely-inspired!)*

10

11   **G'Morin'! Welcome to Channel 64's 'Cookin' with Tulula.'**

12   **I'm Tulula Lee May, your Baptist Gourmet and before I**

13   **lead you in a recipe, I'm gonna lead you in a prayer.**

14   **Lordy, Lordy, let me learn. Not to let my souffle**

15   **burn. And if it does, oh promise me this. Someone in**

16   **my kitchen will like it crisp! Amen.**

17   **Last night, I was divinely inspired when the Lord**

18   **came to me in a dream and He said, 'Tulula, you are my**

19   **culinary link to humanity. I bestow upon you the**

20   **celestial preparation for fried grits.'**

21   **Ingredients are hominy, cheese, and the life-giving**

22   **energy to all the Lord's creatures ... fat.**

23   **First you must baptize your ingredients.** *(Throws*

24   *water on the ingredients with fervor)* **You're baptized!**

25   **You're baptized! You're baptized!**

26   **Next, we finely chop the hominy and the cheese,**

27   **which I already have done because they won't let me**

28   **have the air time I need.** *(Smiles and winks at a producer*

29   *offstage)* **Isn't that right, Jimmy?** *(Under her breath)*

1   Producer Shmoducer.

2   Then, we take the hominy, the cheese, we put it in
3   a skillet and FRY IT UP! JUST FRY IT UP! IN THE
4   NAME OF THE LORD! JUST FRY IT UP! *(Lightheaded,*
5   *she sits down and fans herself)* Oh, this is gonna be a good
6   one.

7   Now, while we're waitin' for the culinary miracle, like
8   waitin' for the second coming, I'd like to read some of
9   my viewer mail. Preacher Mapplethorpe writes, 'Dear
10   Tulula, thank you for bringing that fried Caesar's salad
11   to the church bazaar last week. Everyone raved over
12   those cute little baby Jesus croutons. And that
13   parmesan cheese looked like snow in the manger!'
14   Amen.

15   Tessie Jo Miller from Duncan Road asks, 'Dear
16   Tulula, what is the rule of thumb in Southern Baptist
17   food preparation?' Tessie, has your cheese dun slid off
18   your cracker? Just slap on some cheese and FRY IT UP!
19   FRY IT UP! IN THE NAME OF THE LORD, JUST FRY IT
20   UP! *(Collapses and fans herself again)* Lord save us all.

21   Letter from Madge Peeker on Winston Lane, 'How do
22   I make my home fried taters taste like yours?' Madge, I
23   seen the way you fry those taters at the church socials.
24   You just chop 'em all up like they was the devil's spawn!
25   With each slice, you must instill goodness and ethics
26   and morality. Handle your taters the way God handles
27   His children and your creation will be as perfect as His.
28   On that note, let's resurrect those grits ... *(She tastes*
29   *them)* Mmmmmmmm, mmmmmmmm, just like the Lord
30   woulda made them.

31   Now, tell your Catholic friends to tune in next week
32   because I'm making fried St. Joan Kabobs! Bye, y'all!

33
34
35

What a Man Weighs
by Sherry Kramer

1   Joan — thirty-five   Female

2

3   *(Joan, a thirty-five-year-old single woman in search of*

4   *adventure, works in the book restoring department of a large*

5   *university library. She's just had a blushing, convulsing,*

6   *gasping kissing marathon with a man who also works in the*

7   *library. Now that the man expects more — and quickly —*

8   *Joan begins to suspect that this fleeting encounter is as good*

9   *as it is ever going to get.)*

10

11   You know what the French say, don't you? The French

12   say it is never as good as it is when you are first

13   climbing the stairs. So ... it was good. Really good. It

14   was fabulous. Thank you. So — I once spent a week

15   with a man named Charles at one of those useless

16   bookbinder conventions — everybody sharing the recipe

17   for the perfect non-binding glue, that sort of thing. It

18   was spring, which in France means one thing, but in

19   Nebraska, it means another. It means tornadoes. So,

20   when the convention was over, our plane took off right

21   into the middle of one. Half of all the really big guns in

22   book conservation were on the plane, and I was

23   imagining the headlines if it went down. LIBRARIANS

24   PAY THE BIG FINE. And, PLANE OVERDUE. That sort

25   of thing. I was having an excellent time.

26   I knew that to die with that week I had spent with

27   Charles inside me — to die, not full of fear, or longing,

28   or regret, but full of that — that would be heaven. I don't

29   believe in heaven, do you? The French do, I suppose.

1   But the airplane is an American invention. Which
2   explains a lot of things. Anyway, I didn't die — so much
3   for my one shot at heaven — and, since staircases don't
4   crash — we have to take responsibility ourselves. You
5   said it is never as good as it is when you are first
6   climbing the stairs. I agree. But the stairs didn't crash.
7   We missed our chance. That was as good as it was ever
8   going to get. Why go on?
9
10
11
12
13
14
15
16
17
18
19
20
21
22
23
24
25
26
27
28
29
30
31
32
33
34
35

The Love Space Demands
by Ntozake Shange

1	Unspecified	Female

2

3   *(This choreopoem — poetry-with-movement — is a subtle, soul-*
4   *searching reflection on the lives of African-American women.*
5   *Written as a dramatic monolog, the excerpt titled "Serial*
6   *Monogamy" examines the possibilities and consequences of*
7   *lust and love, infatuation and intimacy. You may wish to*
8   *include choreographed movement to punctuate the flow of the*
9   *theatrical action.)*

10

11   I think/we should reexamine/serial monogamy
12   is it/one at a time or
13   one for a long time?
14   how
15   does the concept of infinity related to a skilled
16   serial monogamist/& can
17   that person consider a diversionary escapade
18   a serial
19   one night stand?
20   can a consistent
21   serial monogamist
22   have one/several/or myriad relationships
23   that broach every pore of one's body
24   so long as there is no penetration?
25   do we/consider adventurous relentless tongues
26   capable of penetration & if we do
27   can said tongues whip thru us indiscriminately
28   with words/like
29   'hello'

1   'oh, you lookin'good'
2   'you jigglin, baby'
3   cd these be reckless immature violations of
4   serial monogamy?
5   i mean/
6   if my eyes light up cuz
7   some stranger just lets go/caint stop hisself
8   from sayin
9   'yr name must be paradise'
10   if I was to grin or tingle/even get a lil happy/
11   hearin me & paradise/
12   now synonyms
13   does that make me a scarlet woman?
14   if I wear a red dress that makes someone else hot
15   does that put me out the fryin pan & into the
16   fire?
17
18   say/
19   my jade bracelet got hot
20   (which aint possible cuz jade aint
21   jade
22   if it aint cold)
23   but say
24   my jade got lit up & burst offa my wrist
25   & i say/
26   'i gotta find my precious stones
27   cuz they my luck'
28   & he say
29   'luck don't leave it goes where
30   you need it'
31   & I say
32   'i gotta find my bracelet'
33   & he say
34   'you know for actual truth
35   you was wearin this bracelet?'

```
1        & i say
2          'a course, it's my luck'
3                        & he say
4        'how you know?'
5        & i say
6          'cuz
7          i heard my jade
8          flyin thru the air
9          over yr head
10         behind my knees
11         &
12         up under the Japanese lampshade!'
13           & he say
14       'you heard yr jade flyin thru the air??'
15         'yes'
16              i say
17       '& where were they flyin from'
18          he say
19          'from my arm' I say
20          'they got hot & jumped offa my arm'
21       'but/
22       where was yr arm?'
23                   he say
24       & i caint say mucha nothin
25       cuz
26       where my arm was a part a some tremendous
27       current/
28       cd be 'lectricity or niggahs on fire/
29       so where my arm was is where/jade gets hot
30       & does that imply the failure of serial monogamy?
31       do flamin flyin jade stones
32       on a arm/that is a kiss/& a man who knows where/
33       luck is
34       take the serial/outta monogamy/& leave
35       love?
```

Why I Hate Being Six Years Old
by A. C. Felicity Kozik

1   Amanda — six   Female

2

3   *(Amanda, a youthful and spontaneous child, offers a carefully*

4   *drawn sketch of her six-year-old life based on actual events*

5   *and commonplace observations! She is a very serious young*

6   *lady with a clear sense of direction and purpose. Although*

7   *there is anguish in Amanda's tone, it should not detract from*

8   *the spirit of good fun and humor to be found in a child's*

9   *independent, personal values.)*

10

11   Adults always go through these things called Mid-Life

12   Crisis. Grown-ups do nothing but complain about being

13   grown-ups and how their lives are so complicated. Lots

14   of old people say things like, 'How good it would be to

15   be a kid again ... ' and 'I've gotten in touch with my

16   inner child.' Me and my best friend Stu have

17   summarized our dilemma as an 'Early-Life Crisis.' Don't

18   laugh at me, 'Early-Life Crisis' are going to be the next

19   discovery.

20   First off, I'm six years old and yet all my relatives

21   believe I'm a huge Barney fanatic. For Kindergartners,

22   Barney is way uncool. While we're on the subject of

23   kid's shows, let me just state that Power Rangers are

24   not as popular as grown-ups think they are. For school

25   this year my dad got me a pink lunch box. Adults seem

26   to think ALL little girls love that color. Personally, it

27   makes me gag. After I protested getting a Barbie for my

28   fifth birthday my parents gave me a G.I. Joe. Listen, I'm

29   into Legos, not frilly dolls, not war crazy action figures.

Next thing I'd like to share, cooties. It's hard to feel secure as a child when the cootie spread is worse than ever. My mom swears cooties are made-up things hypo-c-cc-con-dria — . I forget the word, that the hypo people made up. Yesterday Billy kissed Susie, two hours later Susie came down with a near fatal case of the chicken pox. Trust me as a kid, cooties exist and remain as a deadly threat in elementary schools.

I could go on forever why being a kid is so tuff, but I think we've touched two of the most important issues today, lame adult ignorance and hazardous cooties. Ever since me and Stu started telling our classmates about the 'Early Life Crisis' everyone calls me the doctor. If you need me I'll be revising some files of my friends, with purple and red crayon, in my room. Ba-bye!

Sister Santa
by Jim Chevallier

1   Sister Santa — age unspecified   Female

2

3   *(A dark parody of the Yuletide hero Santa Claus, Sister Santa*
4   *is a sour and impatient holiday elf. There are no warm*
5   *moments of holiday cheer or reminiscences of the good old*
6   *Christmas spirit here! Sister Santa has a mocking tone as she*
7   *taunts and sneers at the startled children standing in line to*
8   *visit. Her impolite conversation signals the comic response*
9   *that follows.)*

10

11   Ho, ho, ho!

12   I am too Santa Claus, kid. Yeah, I'm a girl. Like duh-
13   uh. Because I need the money, O.K.? It's either you little
14   germ-donors or cooking Christmas burgers at the local
15   take-out.

16   Hey, but enough about me. What greedy little totally
17   unreasonable demand do you want to make of the Great
18   White Beard? No, I didn't grow the beard. I'm a girl,
19   O.K.? We don't as a general thing grow beards. Hey,
20   look, would you rather have me or some red-eyed wino
21   who's working off his last bottle of Boone's Farm? Like
22   liquor-breath, do you? Well, then, work with me here,
23   O.K.? I got midterms next week plus a female problem
24   you don't want to know about, so trust me, I am not in
25   the mood.

26   What'll it be then? A molded plastic semi-automatic
27   so you can imitate your favorite mad gunman? Some
28   bloodthirsty boy-doll that crawls around on its belly,
29   armed to the teeth? A little remote control tank you can

1   send shooting through pedestrians' feet and scare the
2   Pampers off frail old ladies? Come on, sweetie, you just
3   tell Sister Santa here what violence and mayhem
4   disguised as a toy will put your little testosterone-tainted
5   heart all a flutter. Rat-a-tat-tat! Boom, boom, boom!
6   No, I do NOT have a problem with men! Where do
7   you get this stuff? What kind of shows do your parents
8   let you watch, anyway? And no there is nothing weird
9   about a female Santa! You better get used to it, kid,
10   when you grow up, there's gonna be girls EVERYWHERE!
11   Yeah, that's right, we're even in the Army!
12   Ah no, now I've gone and made you cry. Hey, can we
13   get a nurturer over here?
14   Anyone into being maternal?
15   Geez ...
16
17
18
19
20
21
22
23
24
25
26
27
28
29
30
31
32
33
34
35

The Indelicate Instructor
by Rev. Jay Goldstein

1   Instructor — age unspecified   Male

2

3   *(A devoted third grade teacher sets very high standards for his*

4   *class, and treats the children as if they were older than they are.*

5   *He is filled with colorful language and holds his attentive students*

6   *spell-bound with classroom antics. In this abbreviated lesson plan,*

7   *the indelicate instructor percolates in a satiric tirade that youthful*

8   *and unsuspecting children could not possibly comprehend.)*

9

10   OK class ... OK ... OK. Calm yourselves. OK, quiet,

11   better, good. Eyes front. You are in third grade you're not

12   little second graders and I expect you all to act as adults.

13   Now class, I'm sure you noticed that Tammy did not

14   come back from lunch with the rest of you. I sent her to

15   the office so we could talk about her behind her back. It

16   has come to my attention that many of you have been

17   making fun of Tammy both on the playground and in gym

18   class. Children, she can not help the way she looks. It is

19   not her fault that her face was smoothed away in a freak

20   sandpaper accident. It will not help the situation by

21   calling her 'Tammy no-face' and chanting 'Got your nose.'

22   It was an accident and we should not burden her with

23   personal responsibility no matter how annoying she is or

24   how stupid something is that she does. *(Abruptly stops)*

25   OK class, on your desk should be a book. Do not

26   open it until I tell you. This book is called *I Can Read* and

27   you will be responsible for its return at the end of the

28   year in good reading condition. I will expect you to

29   return this book in exactly as you received it. I don't

1   expect to see ripped pages, or 'dog-eared' pages and I
2   certainly don't want to catch any of you writing in the
3   book. Grown-ups do not write in our books.
4   Now open the front cover of your books, take your
5   pencil and write your name. Does everyone have a
6   pencil? No, yes, no? If you don't have a pencil borrow one
7   from a neighbor. Everyone have a pencil? No, yes, no?
8   Good. Now on the first empty line, write your name, last
9   name first, first name last and middle initial in the
10   margin and fill in the date omitting the first two digits
11   and separate them with a comma. OK everyone. Put
12   your pencils down on your desk. You can finish during
13   free-time if you write a little slow. Pencils down, put
14   them down, put them down. Class, class *(Raises hand)*
15   class, 'When the hand goes up the mouth goes shut.' OK
16   everyone 'When the hand goes up the mouth goes shut.'
17   OK? No, yes, no? Good.
18   Oh hi Tammy, take your seat. Please Tammy, take
19   your seat. Come on hurry up. The longer you take to get
20   to your seat the less time the rest of the class will have
21   at recess. OK? No, yes, no? Good. *(In a eerie, soothing*
22   *tone)* OK everyone open your books to the first chapter
23   and start reading silently the story entitled *Billy Visits*
24   *the Big City.* While you read silently I want you to make
25   sure you can answer these three questions. 'Why does
26   Billy go to the city?', 'What does Billy find in grandpa's
27   underwear drawer?' And for bonus points, 'How does
28   Billy's trip to the big city work as a metaphor for the
29   alienation of the middle class post-industrial America?'
30   Spelling counts. Any questions? No, yes, no? Good.
31   OK class, books open eyes down and read silently.
32   Now while you read I'll be in the teacher's lounge. If you
33   have any questions, Mr. Tong the custodian will be here
34   and I don't want you bothering him about his days in the
35   carnival.

Men & Cars
by Diane Spodarek

1   Maggie — age unspecified   Female

2

3   *(Maggie, a musician and single mother, perches seductively*

4   *on a stool at The Last Exit Bar. There is an air of mystery and*

5   *uncertainty that surrounds her, and it is apparent that she is*

6   *a woman of cunning and seductive charms. Maggie delights*

7   *in the current scandals and intrigues that are making the*

8   *rounds of the city, and here she spins her own tall tale for the*

9   *amusement of the patrons.)*

10

11   I like to drink a tall Bud when I'm walking around the

12   streets of Manhattan. I keep it in a brown paper bag and

13   sip it through a straw. Sometimes I like to stand on the

14   corner and wait. Wait for the men. You ever watch men

15   and their cars? Ever watch men look under their cars? I

16   like the way men look when they look under their cars.

17   I like to watch men sit in their cars, start them up,

18   find out they don't start, get out, look at the car, then

19   go to the hood. Open the hood, look in, go back to the

20   inside of the car, and try to start it up again. Get out

21   again, look under the car, look at the ground, look at the

22   spill on the ground, look all around, sometimes at their

23   companion, if they're with someone. If not, look for

24   another man in the vicinity to share this moment. Then

25   there are two or three sometimes four men looking

26   under the hood or looking under the car, or at the

27   ground. Sometimes they stare at the spill on the ground

28   together, and then they look at each other and they get

29   that look. I like that look. It's somehow familiar. I can't

put my finger on it, I can't really say what it is, but it just gives me a funny feeling watching them, the men and their cars, although I don't really think it has anything to do with the fact that I'm from Detroit.

The Fastest Clock in the Universe
by Philip Ridley

1   Sherbet — seventeen   Female

2

3   *(Sherbet Gravel, a bossy, brassy, seventeen-year-old pregnant*
4   *teenager, is engaged to sixteen-year-old Foxtrot Darling. Foxtrot*
5   *is being pursued by Cougar Glass, a thirty-year-old woman*
6   *who dreams of remaining an eternal teenager. At a birthday*
7   *party for a friend, Sherbet persuades all the guests to reveal*
8   *their "wish" for the future. Her own desire, it seems, is to*
9   *subtly confront the aging Cougar.)*

10

11   Who wants to know my wish? I wish to grow old gracefully.
12   Now I know that sounds ridiculous, but I've seen enough
13   people not doing it gracefully to know what I'm talking
14   about. The beauty salon where I work is full of them. Men
15   and women, all with the same look in their eyes. Make me
16   young, says the look. But you know something? There's
17   nothing we can do. Nature has rules and regulations and
18   most of them are either cruel or very cruel. You know, I
19   can usually tell a person's age as easy as that! One look
20   is all it takes. There's this one woman who comes in — I
21   feel sorry for her in a way — and she's got this photograph
22   of what she looked like when she was nineteen. She must
23   be fifty if she's a day now. Anyway, she comes in and she
24   shows me this photograph and ... was she beautiful! 'This
25   was me,' she says. It's as if that photograph captured her
26   at the happiest moment of her life. Perhaps it's like that.
27   Perhaps we reach our peak when we're nineteen and, for
28   one glorious summer, we're in control of our lives, and we
29   look wonderful and everything is perfect. And then it's
30   never the same again. And we spend the rest of our lives
31   merely surviving one empty summer after another.

Tea
by Velina Hasu Houston

1   Himiko — age unspecified   Female

2

3   *(Himiko, a Japanese "war bride," has committed suicide at*

4   *the beginning of the play. As a group of Japanese women*

5   *married to American servicemen gather to clean Himiko's*

6   *house, she reappears from the netherworld. Himiko wears a*

7   *feminine but mysterious dress over which is a kimono of*

8   *distorted colors. Himiko speaks of her daughter's tragic*

9   *murder, the final blow that led her to take her own life.)*

10

11   I was born in a storm and it's never stopped raining. My

12   only blessing is Mieko, my half-Japanese girl. I love her

13   so much, but she was born in my storm, too. For years,

14   I tried to talk to her, but she wasn't ready. *(A sad laugh)*

15   Mieko is so fast, I only know what she looks like from

16   behind. Because she's always leaving, her big Japanese

17   o-shiri swaying like a flower, out looking for dreams she

18   thinks men are going to give her. So it was a Saturday

19   in May, Mieko wants to make me worry, so she

20   hitchhikes. She's gone three days. Then the big

21   policeman comes. 'Do you have a daughter named

22   Mieko? When's the last time you saw her, Mrs.

23   Hamilton?' *(Breathes hard and fast; forces composure)*

24   The last time I saw Mieko is in the dusk. She looks

25   so Japanese, her shoulders curving like gentle hills.

26   Mieko came home today. Someone made her dirty,

27   stabbed her in the chest many times and then raped her

28   as she died. Left a broom inside my little girls' body. Her

29   brassiere was shredded by the knife. *(A beat)* There is no

1   one for me. There never was. Even my sisters of Japan
2   cannot bless me with sandals to cover my blistered feet
3   as I prepare for the longest journey. *(Looks around)*
4   Billy, is that you? Before it's too late, tell me the
5   truth. You loved me, didn't you? Once. Once there was
6   nobody like me. Now that I know, I can go on without
7   you, Billy. I see you there, waiting in the mist, your
8   strong arms ready to hold me for one last dance. But I'm
9   going another way. Like bamboo. I sway back and forth
10 in the wind, bending but never breaking. Never again.
11 The war is over. Mother? Is that you? Are you waiting for
12 me, too? *(Brief, absolute delight, addressing Mieko when*
13 *she was five)* Mieko-chan, I see you dancing in my best
14 kimono: all light and laughter and ... clean! *(The delight*
15 *fades)* No, you all have to let me go now. I have a long
16 walk ahead of me. All ties are unbound, as completely
17 as if they never existed.
18
19
20
21
22
23
24
25
26
27
28
29
30
31
32
33
34
35

The Madness of Esme and Shaz
by Sarah Daniels

1   Shaz — age unspecified   Female

2

3   *(Shaz, a feisty woman who spent thirteen years in Broadmoor*

4   *Prison for murder, is now in a committed relationship with*

5   *Pat, a younger woman studying for her Ph.D. and working as*

6   *a ticket conductor on British Rail. When Pat invites Shaz to*

7   *live with her, Shaz decides to reveal her past history. Pat*

8   *wrongly assumes that Shaz killed her father, and in this*

9   *confession Shaz sets the record straight.)*

10

11   Three years after I was taken into care my Mother died.

12   I didn't feel anything. I thought. 'That's it then. My

13   Mother's dead.' She'd not visited me in three years. I

14   was in care because she put him before me. *(Without*

15   *looking at her.)* You won't find any easy answers for this

16   in the books you've read. But when she died a feeling of

17   hope went. Anyway several years later my Father

18   married again. They had two children — a boy, and a

19   baby girl. I left care when I was sixteen. You had to. I got

20   a job in an old peoples home. I was — Oh. I don't know.

21   My behavior was rather strange. I used to cut myself. No

22   one ever knew. They told me I was very good at my job.

23   They had no idea. I was — it was like I was very cut off.

24   I decided to look for and found my Father. He was

25   pleased enough to be reunited. I babysat for them. They

26   gave me a key to the house. Sometimes when I knew

27   they were out I would let myself in and write stuff with

28   her lipstick over the mirror. Tip her perfume over the

29   bed. Smear body lotion into the carpet. One evening I

1   was babysitting. *(She stops.)* I murdered the baby. Girl. I
2   picked her up from her crib thing and held her.
3   Squeezed her. Until she stopped breathing. When I knew
4   she was dead, I sat down, turned the television up and
5   waited for them to come home.
6
7
8
9
10
11
12
13
14
15
16
17
18
19
20
21
22
23
24
25
26
27
28
29
30
31
32
33
34
35

Once a Catholic
by Mary O'Malley

1 Father Mullarkey — age unspecified   Male

2

3   *(Father Mullarkey, an imposing figure with remarkable insight*

4   *into modern education, is an invited guest at the convent of*

5   *Our Lady of Fatima. The convent, a grammar school for young*

6   *girls, prides itself on a tradition of spiritual piety. Today is a*

7   *celebration of that tradition, and Father Mullarkey addresses*

8   *the young girls with a good-humored examination of the*

9   *subject of purity.)*

10

11   Now, I want to say a little word to you about the vital

12   importance of purity. You're all getting to be big girls

13   now. Indeed, some of you are bigger than others! Isn't it

14   a great joy to be young and healthy with all your life

15   before you. Sooner or later you might want to share your

16   life with a member of the opposite sex. The best way to

17   find a boyfriend is to join a Catholic Society where you'll

18   have scope of all sorts of social activities. Now, when

19   you've met your good Catholic boy and you're getting to

20   know each other he might suggest a bit of a kiss and a

21   cuddle. Well, let him wait! And if he doesn't want to wait

22   let him go. And cuddling and kissing is bound to arouse

23   bad feelings and desires for the intimate union allowed

24   only in matrimony.

25   *(He bangs on the desk)* The intimate union of the

26   sexes is a sacred act. A duty to be done in a state of

27   grace by a man and his wife and nobody else! So, until

28   the day you kneel at the altar with a bridal veil on your

29   head you must never be left alone in a room with a

1 boyfriend. Or in a field for that matter! Let the two of
2 you go out and about with other young couples to
3 dances and parties and the like. But a particular word
4 of warning about the latter. There's no doubt at all that
5 alcoholic drinks make a party go with a swing. The
6 danger is that after a couple of drinks a boy and a girl
7 are more inclined to take liberties with each other. To
8 indulge in such liberties is sinful. The girl has the special
9 responsibility in the matter because a boy's passions
10 are more readily aroused. God help him!
11   Show your affection by all means. But keep to
12 holding hands with an occasional kiss on the cheek. A
13 Catholic boy, in his heart of hearts, will be impressed by
14 such insistence on perfect chastity. Ask Our Blessed
15 Lady to keep you free from the temptations of the flesh.
16 And make no mistake about it, a passionate kiss on the
17 lips between a boy and a girl is a serious mortal sin. *(He*
18 *bangs on the desk)* When you've the wedding ring on your
19 finger you can fire away to your heart's content! Now,
20 has any girl any question she'd like to ask?
21
22
23
24
25
26
27
28
29
30
31
32
33
34
35

Class Action
by Brad Slaight

1 Dennis — teenager   Male

2

3   *(Dennis, a sensitive teenager with a brilliant mind, is viewed*

4   *as a nerd by his high school classmates. Often a daily object*

5   *of ridicule and scorn, he remains a very serious, mature*

6   *young man with a strong sense of his own personal identity.*

7   *Sitting alone in an empty classroom, Dennis reflects on his life*

8   *as a genius and clings to a spirit of optimism for more*

9   *promising rewards in the real world.)*

10

11   **My name is Dennis Gandleman. Around this school I am**

12   **the object of ridicule from most of the students, simply**

13   **because I have an extremely high I.Q. It's 176. My father**

14   **wanted me to enroll in a special school that deals with**

15   **geniuses like myself, but Mother was firmly against**

16   **that. She wanted me to have a normal education, and**

17   **not be treated as some kind of freak ... Which is ironic,**

18   **because that's exactly what is happening to me here.**

19   **The whole concept of education is a paradox: High**

20   **School is supposed to celebrate education and**

21   **knowledge, but what it really celebrates is social groups**

22   **and popularity. In a perfect world, a kid like me would**

23   **be worshipped because of my scholastic abilities,**

24   **instead of someone who can throw a forty-yard**

25   **touchdown pass. I suppose I could complain, and**

26   **bemoan the unfairness of it all. But I am bright. I know**

27   **something that the others don't ... That, once we leave**

28   **High School and enter the real world, all the rules**

29   **change. What matters is power. Financial power. Power**

1   that comes from making a fortune on cutting-edge
2   computer software. Software that I am already
3   developing. *(Pause.)* **Some call me a nerd. I call myself**
4   **... ahead of my time. See you on the outside.**
5
6
7
8
9
10
11
12
13
14
15
16
17
18
19
20
21
22
23
24
25
26
27
28
29
30
31
32
33
34
35

In Poetic Defence
by Richard Gilbert Hill

1   Lord Byron — age unspecified   Male

2

3   *(The proud and sensuous English romantic poet Lord Byron*

4   *(1788-1824), often wounded by the sad arrows of failed love,*

5   *is the subject of this modern character portrait. The poet's*

6   *chronic pursuit of idealized beauty and love is treated gently*

7   *with a present-day sense of humor. In his reminiscence to a*

8   *friend, Byron shares an awkward encounter in his life and*

9   *affords us a moment of comic pleasure.)*

10

11   In the cold, cold bristly breeze of night off the sea, I sat,

12   my toes exposed to the lapping waves that bit like frogs

13   with teeth. My shoes were lost, thrown to the farthest

14   leap of my arm that I might lose my way without feet

15   enclosed by cheap leather and soles. Mad I was that

16   night, and the stars meant nothing, and the beach

17   meant nothing, and I stared with bitter eyes into the

18   dark, dark crashing sounds of water on rock. I kept

19   praying for warmth: her small hands fondling me, her

20   tongue licking my lips and teasing me with her voice.

21   But I couldn't rid my inner mind of the truths I know life

22   to be. Like clocks are for time and schedules for lovers

23   to keep, not careers and parties where anything can

24   happen with someone else. The laughter of ugly pug

25   people singed my ears from up the sandy way where talk

26   was seductive and leering.

27   Too many rich people for my taste, the fast set with

28   big houses and boats, with greed in their guts trying to

29   feed themselves with bodies like tombs. Soul-less

1   creatures with little to show for their money but lies.
2   And she cavorted with them, and danced in the firelight.
3   Enticed by their talk, spun in their words, she looked for
4   opportunities. I fell in love with a fool and I was more the
5   fool for it. Against my mind's wishes, my heart ached for
6   her and my body was as tense as my thoughts. So I sat
7   and waited to see who would come to me first: the love
8   of my life or the tide. *(Beat)* She was a sweet, pretty girl,
9   her head full of golden curls and a laugh that sparkled.
10   She wore short skirts and small shoes and moved in a
11   way that gave rhythm to music. And so she was worth
12   waiting for. And I got water up my rear end doing just
13   that. Waiting. A numbness set in that I still haven't
14   recovered from. I walk stiffly now, but I hold my head
15   erect, for certainly nothing else is these days. And I
16   chatter myself up with congratulations for such a
17   dramatic exit from her life, ultimately spending the night
18   with the homeless. Poetic, I thought. Absolutely poetic.
19
20
21
22
23
24
25
26
27
28
29
30
31
32
33
34
35

Medea
by Christopher Durang and Wendy Wasserstein

1   Actress — age unspecified   Female

2

3   *(This light-hearted sketch, loosely based on Euripides' classical*

4   *tragedy* The Trojan Women, *takes place on the stage of a*

5   *drama school and features a highly animated actress who*

6   *speaks as a chorus-figure to open the play. The range of present-*

7   *day subjects treated is broad and rather crudely parodied. The*

8   *actress is in reckless high spirits and provides a good-humored*

9   *introduction to the savage lampoon that follows.)*

10

11   Hello. I am she who will be Medea. That is, I shall play

12   the heroine from that famous Greek tragedy by

13   Euripides for you. I attended a first-rate School of

14   Dramatic Arts. At this wonderful school, I had classical

15   training, which means we start at the very beginning, a

16   very good place to start. Greek tragedy. How many of

17   your lives are Greek tragedy? Is Olympia Dukakis here

18   this evening? As an actress who studies the classics,

19   one of the first things you learn in drama school is that

20   there are more roles for men than for women. This is a

21   wonderful thing to learn because it is true of the real

22   world as well. Except for *Thelma and Louise.* At drama

23   school, in order to compensate for this problem, the

24   women every year got to act in either *The Trojan Women*

25   or *The House of Bernardo Alba.* This prepared us for bit

26   parts in *Designing Women* and *Little House on the*

27   *Prairie.* Although these shows are canceled now, and we

28   have nothing to do. Tonight, we would like to present to

29   you a selection from one of the most famous Greek

1 tragedies ever written, *The Trojan Women.* Our scene is
2 directed by Michael Cacoyannis and choreographed by
3 June Taylor. And now, translated from the Greek by
4 George Stephanoulous, here is a scene from this
5 terrifying tragedy.
6
7
8
9
10
11
12
13
14
15
16
17
18
19
20
21
22
23
24
25
26
27
28
29
30
31
32
33
34
35

Woman
by Swati Pandey

1   Woman — age unspecified   Female

2

3   *(An obsessive woman vents her anger and hostility in a*

4   *psychotic act of brutality and murder. The long-suffering*

5   *culprit voices her outrage and sense of rejection in a stream*

6   *of bitter curses against the man she has just killed. In an*

7   *almost cinematic retelling of the events, the woman appears*

8   *so distracted that one might question her sanity or fear she*

9   *may do harm to herself.)*

10

11   i think about him. i think about him again and again.

12   how he walks and how he leans against the wall — his

13   wall — thinking about something, something only he

14   knows and only he feels. his eyes fog over when he

15   enters his little world. they're fogged over right now.

16   well, he sure is in another world. but it ain't anywhere

17   near this one. yeah, its pretty far away i would suppose.

18   he never looked at me. not once would he ever turn and

19   gaze into my eyes. he looked over my shoulder, above

20   my head, past me, next to me. everywhere else but in

21   my eyes. and i hated him. but i was in love.

22   why didn't he notice me? it was like i wasn't there.

23   and every once in a while when i saw him smile, i knew

24   he wasn't smiling at me. or for me. it was for someone

25   else.

26   anyway, it really wasn't his fault. it was hers. she

27   had long beautiful hair and she was tall and perfect in

28   every way. everything i wasn't. and she had him. and i

29   was more lonely than ever. i'd sit there staring at the

1   alcohol in my cabinet. which i didn't touch ... not often.

2   and i'd think of him and her together going out and

3   laughing. things i'd left behind. it's like a disease to be

4   lonely. i didn't feel like doing anything and my mind, it

5   focused on one thing. him.

6   well i finally got his attention. yeah. i made him look

7   at me. i went up to him one day and stood right in front

8   of him. looking ugly and hideous as usual, but he didn't

9   dare turn away. i held the gun straight up to his

10   forehead and said, come with me. how could he refuse

11   me? *(smiles)* so he got into my car and i made like we

12   were going on a date and chatted with him about

13   charming subjects. not boring like the weather or

14   something like that. i came off as very intelligent. yes,

15   he was enchanted by me. i drove him home in my beat

16   up little car to my beat up little house. i picked up the

17   gun and fingered the trigger, gently caressing it like an

18   old friend. i invited him inside. i said, oh do sit down,

19   sir, while i make us both comfortable. all the time

20   holding the gun in my hand. i suppose that didn't make

21   him very comfortable. i brought us champagne and set

22   it down and we drank and laughed together. of course i

23   did most of the talking! the boy was scared stiff of me!

24   he must have been a tad nervous, in a lady's home and

25   everything, not knowing quite how to approach the

26   situation. yes ... *(musing)* the confidence was all a put-

27   on. it was his first time.

28   i took him down to my basement where the stone

29   walls are cold and silent. i told him that here in this

30   room he would know how i sat at home and in bed and

31   cried over him. nights and nights of longing, wasting my

32   life away yearning for things i couldn't have. that i

33   wasn't good enough to have. and why, why wasn't i good

34   enough? beautiful people who walk with their heads held

35   high in disgust of the ugliness at their feet. he got a little

scared then. *(laughs)* he was a gentleman to the end. never laid a hand on me. *(smile disappears)* never laid a hand on me.

   i killed him. i killed a man. i poured my heart out to him and then i killed him. how I'd longed to have someone to share my troubles, and someone to listen to me, but no one did. until he came and finally i had someone to listen to me, with a bit of persuasion. so as i held the gun to his forehead and finished my long sad tale of bars and disgrace, i knew he was the cause. he made me what i am. a sick old woman. a maniac. it was him! he knew what he was doing all along. i had been the victim of a twisted game. he wanted to see me hurt. he went to her so i would be hurt. he never looked at me so i would know how unbearable i was.

   so i killed him. i did it, and now he's in my basement. right now. lying in a pool of his own blood. imagine that he's here in my own home. he's finally where i've always wanted him. he keeps me company now. i still look at him. sitting on the floor, leaned up against a wall — his wall — in his own little world.

Faith in Flowers
by Shannon M. Scheel

1   Laura — young girl   Female

2

3   *(Laura, a lively young girl wearing dirty jeans, ripped T-shirt,*

4   *and a soiled apron, enters hurriedly carrying a bucket and a*

5   *flower. She crosses to center stage with a sense of urgency,*

6   *puts the bucket down and looks about ready to scrub the*

7   *floor. Laura speaks directly to the audience and gives a brief*

8   *glimpse of her career prospects. She is an enticing free-spirit*

9   *with considerable charm.)*

10

11   Oh, hi! I didn't see you there! Welcome to Mr.

12   Fernwick's Flower Haven! My name is Laura, how can I

13   brighten your life today? *(Giggles)* Okay, that is corny I'll

14   admit, but my boss, Jim, says I have to say it to every

15   customer ... not like we get many these days. Why's

16   that? 'Cause it's the new millennium! Nobody really

17   gives flowers anymore. I mean, for example, my sister,

18   Erika, works at that fancy electronics store down the

19   block.

20   Every night at dinner she tells me stories of how

21   husbands or boyfriends come in and buy a romantic CD

22   to apologize for a fight with their sweetie, or how a nine-

23   year old boy walks in with a wad of cash to buy mommy

24   a new DVD player for her birthday. He gets it from his

25   dad who's in the next aisle over. I don't think a

26   lemonade stand could make four hundred fifty dollars

27   and ninety-nine cents ... it just isn't possible, you

28   know? But for four dollars and fifty cents, he can buy her

29   a nice bouquet all by himself. I know my mom would

1   appreciate that more. I mean, I don't believe anyone has
2   faith in flowers anymore.
3   But enough about me, what can I do for you? We
4   have this great special on lilacs. You get two for ... huh?
5   *(Long pause)* Oh, I don't know if he's in ... *(Calls into the*
6   *back)* Jim? Jim? The landlord's here. He said that if you
7   don't have the rent today ... Jim? He's not here,
8   apparently. Please, if you just wait until tomorrow ... !
9   Oh, you've been waiting for a month ... Well, yes I
10   understand. The computer place bought us out ... I see
11   ... Yes, I'll lock up ... *(Takes the flower from her pocket and*
12   *places it on the table)* Here ... a freebie ... If you put it in
13   water right away, it'll keep for a while. Makes a nice
14   centerpiece. You're welcome ... and thanks for stopping
15   by! *(Wipes her hands on the apron)* Now to start packing
16   up, and ... what's this? *(Picks up paper on the table and*
17   *reads)* 'Now hiring: Virtual Boutique Inc — send your
18   loved ones gifts online for half the cost ... ' *(Smirks)* Huh
19   ... welcome to the twenty-first century.
20
21
22
23
24
25
26
27
28
29
30
31
32
33
34
35

The Soy Answer
by Carolyn West

1   Amber Johanson — age unspecified   Male/Female
2
3   *(In this dark, brittle spoof of zombies and vampires, the*
4   *resourceful entrepreneur Amber Johanson is pitching vegan*
5   *health food to the grateful undead. As a sales representative*
6   *for Soy Answers, Inc., the quirky Amber is quick to point out*
7   *the nutritional value of the product and offer a test sample to*
8   *the kindred spirits. The tone is deliciously sinister and the*
9   *character portrait side-splitting in its cleverness.)*
10
11   How many zombies are here tonight? That's a good
12   number. I know how your day goes. You get up in the
13   evening and right away you're starving. You're craving
14   human brains. Now it's a fact that zombies need the
15   nutrition from a fresh brain. You can't have the canned
16   or pickled kind. So the first thing you do when you get
17   up is track down breakfast. My goodness, you're
18   exhausted. You've just dug yourself out of your grave.
19   You don't have the energy to go hunting. I have the
20   solution. Tofu Brains. It has all the nutrition you need
21   and tofu stays fresh without preservatives for an
22   amazingly long time. Tofu also has astonishing health
23   benefits. Recent studies show that women who eat tofu
24   three times a day are at a much lower risk for ovarian
25   cancer. That's something to think about. And before
26   you raise your hands, I know you're already thinking
27   about the taste. Rest assured, the flavor is just
28   wonderful. It even has the texture of gray matter. We've
29   done taste tests all over the country. We gave people

1   Tofu Brains and the real thing and they could not tell the
2   difference. In fact, in just a moment I'm going to give
3   you the same taste test. I have human brains and I have
4   Tofu Brains and I'm not going to tell you which is which.
5
6
7
8
9
10
11
12
13
14
15
16
17
18
19
20
21
22
23
24
25
26
27
28
29
30
31
32
33
34
35

The Mysterious Speck
by Emily Picha

1   Wendy Badoosh — older woman   Female

2

3   *(Wendy Badoosh, a mature but slightly balding woman, enters*

4   *with a flourish wearing a color-clashing 1980's outfit and a*

5   *scary hair style! She is a madcap eccentric who freely offers her*

6   *personal views on life as well as UFO's. Wendy's latest*

7   *misadventure is solving the secret of "the mysterious speck,"*

8   *and she is relentless in the pursuit of an answer to this puzzling,*

9   *unsolved riddle.)*

10

11   **I was outside weeding the tomato bed, and all of a sudden**

12   **I see this weird speck of light on my shed. You know, the**

13   **kind of light that happens when things reflect off the sun**

14   **and stuff. Well, I get distracted. You know me, hah! I get**

15   **really distracted by THAT kind of stuff. Well other kinds of**

16   **stuff, like when my cat is cleaning herself. I stop whatever**

17   **I am doing and watch this miracle. I wish I could do that.**

18   *(Attempts to clean herself· with her paw, licking and then*

19   *rubbing on her forehead like a cat.)* **I mean cats are reeeeeaaly**

20   **cool in that respect Dogs don't do that, they just lick.**

21   **They don't have the style or the grace that our little feline**

22   **snugglepoofs have. Grace! Oh my god I almost forgot. It's**

23   **secretaries day! What am I doing here. Oh, yeah! I came to**

24   **this big building today to tell all these men about my UFO**

25   **experience with the flashing light! I didn't know what it**

26   **was! I was so freaked out. I could be one of those people**

27   **who go on those shows with that UNSOLVED MYSTERIES**

28   **guy and oh my god! I would be such a hit. Those kinds of**

29   **things never happen in daylight. If you want them to**

1   happen in daylight, well they won't. They happen at night.
2   And people don't see so well at night, so ya know, you have
3   to be a cat to really get the vision right. You all know that
4   cats have night vision, right? Well they do. They really do. I
5   mean they can see their paws and know exactly where to
6   clean. That's amazing to me. If it were pitch dark I would
7   probably end up whacking off my nose. My nose is so big.
8   It has exactly three warts and a bunch of blackheads. You
9   know I thought blackheads would disappear when you
10 turned 30, but they don't. Ha! When you're thirty you are
11 just about balding. You know maybe my warts have
12 something to do with this UFO experience. *(Scratches her*
13 *thigh, pauses and looks left for ten seconds, cocking her head in*
14 *an Egyptian-like way.)* Oh my goodness! It moves whenever
15 I move my head. This is ridiculous. They are after me. I
16 have to get my cat here to chase after this space-tinkerbell.
17 I really do have to go on UNSOLVED MYSTERIES now. You
18 guys even have this on film. Uh ... hey, what are you
19 laughing at? *(Stares at an imaginary light bolting wherever her*
20 *head moves on the wall for the rest of the monolog. Eventually*
21 *begins to run around the stage.)*
22   It's my socks, right? They are too normal for you. Not
23 in style enough for you. That's it right? White equals not
24 right, not bright, that is what Fab Fashion's February
25 1986th edition is saying. I subscribe to that. I have six
26 issues. One even talks about what to wear when you are
27 gardening. And for authentic purposes, I wore it. Just so
28 maybe the UFO would come back. And it did, look!
29 LOOK! LOOK! My acre of tomatoes is going to grow,
30 grow, grow! I bet that ... I bet that the space-tinkerbell
31 blessed it. I bet that the space-tinkerbell blessed ME!
32 Now I will never age, never grow bald, never be out of
33 style. I will be so hip! *(Continues to run around the stage as*
34 *lights fade out.)*
35

After the Garden
by Robert J. Lee

1 This partner audition scene should challenge two
2 performers to make performance choices that give
3 contemporary life and meaning to the Biblical characters
4 Adam and Eve. The sample script shows the conflicting
5 first impressions of each character and provides ample
6 opportunities to display vocal variety and subtle
7 movement. There are moments of gentle humor mixed
8 with sober reality that suggest the bonds uniting Adam and
9 Eve. It is important to be aware of the emerging sense of
10 independence and urgency voiced by the characters as
11 they seek their own self-expression. In playing the scene,
12 you should explore spontaneous facial and physical
13 expressions that help clarify Adam and Eve's actions.

14
15 Adam — age unspecified   Male
16 Eve — age unspecified   Female
17
18 *(Adam and Eve stumble forward from behind some bushes*
19 *and face each other center stage. Eve has a look of agitated*
20 *displeasure and Adam wears a frown of disillusionment. The*
21 *downcast look and appearance mirrors their isolation*
22 *following expulsion from the Garden of Eden. They slowly*
23 *begin to confront the elements and the harsh reality of being*
24 *flesh-and-blood human beings.)*
25
26 ADAM: Well, this will be a good excuse to do some
27   traveling. Don't get me wrong the garden was nice and
28   all but it's good for us to get away together. Which way
29   should we go first? How about west? *(Points toward*

1   *audience. EVE keeps walking)* **Okay, north is good. Eve,**
2   **you haven't said two words in the past four hours. Is**
3   **there something wrong?** *(Silence)* **Are you mad?** *(EVE*
4   *stops. Turns and glares at him)* **What's wrong? Did I do**
5   **something?** *(Tries to take her hand but she jerks it away)*
6   **What did I do?** *(EVE turns and heads stage left)* **Come on**
7   **you've got to at least let me know what I did wrong? Did**
8   **I say something wrong?** *(Stops and stares)* **What?**
9 EVE: You know what you said.
10 ADAM: How should I know what I said if you won't tell me?
11 EVE: I might just never speak to you again.
12 ADAM: What did I say?
13 EVE: *(Mockingly)* **That woman You gave me, she gave me of**
14   **the tree, and I ate.**
15 ADAM: I didn't say that.
16 EVE: You most certainly did!
17 ADAM: I did not.
18 EVE: Look it up.
19 ADAM: Huh?
20 EVE: Genesis 3:12
21 ADAM: Okay, but I didn't really mean it like it sounded. I
22   only meant that ...
23 EVE: Don't try to weasel your way out of it. You never want
24   to give me credit for helping, but just let one little thing
25   go wrong and ...
26 ADAM: One little thing huh? You call breaking the only rule
27   we had one little thing?
28 EVE: Not so fast there buster. Who told you, you had to
29   listen to me in the first place? Did I hold you down and
30   shove that fruit down your throat?
31 ADAM: So I thought I told you not to hang around with the
32   serpent.
33 EVE: Well, he tricked me.
34 ADAM: Well there you go then. I wonder why he didn't come
35   around trying to tempt me?

1 EVE: Probably because he figured you couldn't reach the
2   fruit.
3 ADAM: Hey wait a minute!
4 EVE: But besides, who said this was about me? Don't you
5   try to change the subject.
6 ADAM: Uh not so loud Eve. We really shouldn't be fighting
7   like this in front of the kids.
8 EVE: We don't have any kids.
9 ADAM: Oh. That's right. Well ...
10 EVE: So if you think you can humiliate me in front of God
11   like that and get away with it you've got another thing
12   coming Mister. Not even a thought to my feelings.
13 ADAM: But Honey ...
14 EVE: Don't you 'But Honey' me, you ...
15 ADAM: But Sugar if you'll just ... *(Tries to take her hand)*
16 EVE: I wouldn't let you touch me if you were the only man
17   on ... Oh. Well never mind, just keep your hands off
18   me.
19 ADAM: Come on Eve, how long are you going to stay mad
20   like this? *(Eve is silent)* Look, I'll make it up to you.
21 EVE: Hmmph!
22 ADAM: Well ... I'll toil the ground for you. You won't have to
23   do any of the dirty stuff.
24 EVE: Sure like that's your idea. We both know that God's
25   making you do that. Tell you what ... How about if we
26   change assignments. I'll toil the earth and
27   you give birth in pain.
28 ADAM: *(Thinks)* I don't know, don't you think He's mad at
29   us enough as it is?
30 EVE: *(Grudgingly)* Yeah you're right.
31 ADAM: OK, look I won't leave clothes lying around and I'll
32   sweep the dirt. I won't make any mother-in-law jokes.
33   Just please give me a hug.
34 EVE: Can I name the kids?
35 ADAM: Well, I don't know ...

1 EVE: Hey, you got to name all the animals!
2 ADAM: You weren't even here yet! I was handling everything
3   all by myself y'know. *(Under his breath)* **Sure was**
4   **peaceful.**
5 EVE: What was that?
6 ADAM: Oh uh, I was just reminding myself how lonely it
7   was. Okay Honey, how 'bout if we name the kids
8   together.
9 EVE: Well, okay. But I get to name the first one.
10 ADAM: How about we flip for it. C'mon let's go talk about
11   baby names. Hey, what's for dinner? *(Heads stage left)*
12 EVE: *(Watches him leave, shakes her head)* **That woman You**
13   **gave me!**
14 ADAM: Why is this itching so much? Aaughh! Eve, where
15   did you get these leaves?
16 EVE: *(Faces audience with mischievous grin and then heads off*
17   *stage)* **Adam? What's a mother-in-law?**
18
19
20
21
22
23
24
25
26
27
28
29
30
31
32
33
34
35

VOICES OF DESPAIR AND DOUBT

Voices of Despair and Doubt

These voices of despair and doubt paint incisive portraits in which characters struggle to resolve conflicts between duty to oneself and duty to others. Their despair and doubt is traumatic and turbulent at times, but there is no temptation to glorify or idealize the pain and the suffering that surfaces. There is a sense of "photographic realism" reflected in the characters that captures the everyday action and attitude of authentic people as if they had been recorded on a video camera. The result is a pictorial album of life-like portraits drawn from the workaday world of average people who suffer from inner conflicts, neurosis, dysfunctional behavior, or mood depression. Many of the sketches are grim and sober, but there are also moments of unexpected humor to suggest the close bonds that exist between tragedy and comedy.

In playing these voices, you should speak in a conversational tone and move in a natural, relaxed manner. There is a minimum of overt action here, so look for the "inner" truth of each character within the lines of dialog. Be aware of the fierce sense of urgency voiced by the characters as they share intimate confidences and confessions. It may be a useful rehearsal strategy to recall your own personal, sacred catalog of childhood memories, adolescent scars, and wishful dreams to help express the emotional intensity of these voices.

Suicide
by Y York

1   Sylvia — young woman   Male/Female

2

3   *(Sylvia, a young woman who unsuccessfully attempted suicide,*

4   *is now committed to a hospital for observation. She is surrounded*

5   *by other patients who have also faced life-or-death questions and*

6   *offers her advice to those who wish to listen. In a daring defense*

7   *of her own attempt at self-destructive, Sylvia raises sensitive*

8   *questions about the ethical dimensions of suicide.)*

9

10   You screw it up and you don't get a second chance. Nobody

11   trusts you. Doesn't matter what you say. You say, 'Listen,

12   I'm not going to do it again.' You say, 'Listen. I'm not.

13   Going to do it. Again.' You can say, 'No, no. My life is really

14   worth living; I'd never do it again.' That is if you can say

15   that without gagging. Doesn't matter. They don't trust you.

16   They say they do, but suddenly, you're never alone. Used

17   to be people went out to dinner together. Now they go

18   separately, and one of them comes and stays with you.

19   Forget the bathroom. 'Shave your legs? Over my dead

20   body.' They used to knock at a door, but now they just

21   stick their head in to 'see how you are.' They think a head

22   doesn't count, not like walking in with a whole body. For a

23   whole body, they'll knock, but a head they'll send along

24   unannounced.

25   Count. You can't reach four sentences in any

26   conversation before the other person brings it up. 'I'm really

27   sorry about unintelligible mumble.' And if they don't, you do

28   it yourself, out of some perverse guilt. 'Yes, I'm the one, yes,

29   it was razor blades on the wrist. Gillette. Yeah they still

1   make them. It's actually more ecological than using
2   disposable blades. Yes, it did hurt. So badly that it made me
3   really want to live.' Letmeoutletmeoutletmeoutletmeout.
4   Everybody wants to talk about it. Fine, let' em. But what
5   they mean is they want me to talk about it. In a group. Go
6   over and and over it, and every other flawed detail of my
7   over-long existence. And I must listen to others. Failed in
8   life and failed in death. A cry for help? Yes, in some cases,
9   yes. A big cry of 'Look at me, I'm in pain.' That is so
10 optimistic. 'Look at me, I'm in pain, and I think it will go
11 away if I only take the right pill, meet the right person, get
12 the right job, win lotto.' I don't think for a second it will get
13 better. I just screwed up, I screwed it up. Everybody was
14 supposed to be away for the weekend but there was a bomb
15 scare and they all came back to our place to have a party.
16 I screwed up the party too. They were so surprised; nobody
17 was expecting it, nobody knew. And that's the problem.
18 They think because they didn't know that anything was
19 wrong then, why should they think that something isn't
20 wrong now. So, here I sit, practicing until I get it right, or
21 they get bored: 'Listen. I'm not going to do it again. I'm not,
22 I'm not. I'm really not.'
23
24
25
26
27
28
29
30
31
32
33
34
35

Grace Notes
by Rachel Rubin Ladutke

1   Catherine — young woman   Female

2

3   *(Catherine, a young woman who has just given her baby up for*

4   *adoption, sits at a table with her younger sister, Emily. She is*

5   *haunted by recurring headaches and nightmares, and stares*

6   *blankly into open space. Catherine is hopelessly adrift now, forever*

7   *lonely and lost. There is a profound sense of despair in her struggle*

8   *to cope with the brutal torment that has followed her pregnancy.)*

9

10 Every time I get to sleep, I keep having the same dream.

11 I'm walking through this long hallway, and there's nobody

12 else around. Except, I'm walking a little dog. It's really

13 friendly and it loves me. All of a sudden this door opens —

14 I didn't even see it. It's at the end of the hall, right in front

15 of me. There's a really bright light, and voices, and I start

16 feeling faint. The next thing I know, I wake up and the dog

17 is gone. Just when I open my eyes, I hear the door slam

18 shut. As soon as I feel like I can get up, I turn the knob,

19 but it won't open. I try and try, but the door's locked tight.

20   I start crying and screaming, and then I see a window

21 and I notice it's snowing out. So I go outside, and I start

22 dancing in the snow. I feel so free, I can almost forget about

23 losing the dog. Off in the distance I see a little building,

24 and I start running towards it. When I get close enough, I

25 see that it's an animal shelter, and I realize what I really

26 want is to get another dog. But the woman in the shelter

27 says I can't. Somehow she knows I felt happy when the dog

28 disappeared, and she tells me I don't deserve another one.

29 I beg and beg her, and finally she agrees to let me look at

1   their dogs. But I can't find any like the one I lost. And that's
2   the only one I want. I start crying. Then I wake up, and I'm
3   really crying.

4   I don't remember much about giving birth, but I know I
5   heard her cry. I didn't get to look at her, or hold her. The
6   nurse even said I didn't deserve to see her because I was
7   giving her away. They did let me feed her once. I had to
8   refuse to sign the papers before they'd even let me do that.
9   She had blue eyes. I think most babies have blue eyes, but
10   hers weren't at all pale. They were really deep, deep blue.
11   Like the ocean. One hour, that's all we had together. Then
12   they took her away again.

13   You know what I really don't get, Emmy? When I talked
14   to the other girls at the agency, they all kept saying they
15   couldn't wait to give birth so they could get back to normal.
16   But I didn't want to have the baby, because then I was
17   going to lose her. I tried to keep her with me as long as I
18   could. I started having pains in the middle of the night, but
19   I didn't wake Mom up until I couldn't stand it any more. I
20   didn't want to go to the hospital, 'cause I knew I'd be
21   coming home alone and empty. That's the worst part, I
22   think. I feel so empty. I'm cold all the time.

23   And now everyone expects me to just go on like nothing
24   happened. They lied to me. Nobody told me it would be like
25   this. I'm not even twenty years old, Emily, and I feel like my
26   life is over. And I just keep waiting for it to stop hurting.
27   But it doesn't. It just gets worse. You don't know how much
28   it hurts. Emmy.

29   Hold me?

30

31

32

33

34

35

Scene of Shipwreck
by Pamela Mills

1	Daphne — thirties	Female

2

3 *(Daphne, a woman in her thirties, and her younger sister, Ruth,*
4 *were both violated as children by their father. The "unspeakable*
5 *acts" were surely known by family members, but there has been*
6 *a conspiracy of silence to keep the past a buried secret. Daphne*
7 *now describes an argument with her abusive ex-husband Robert*
8 *to an older Ruth. Robert, however, is a fiction — an escapist*
9 *game that Daphne plays to keep herself sane.)*

10

11 When we first met, Robert was so sweet. He used to bring
12 me flowers every time. He was always so considerate. Once
13 I was wearing a dress and he said, 'I don't think you should
14 be wearing that.' I said, 'But it's the fashion — everyone's
15 wearing this kind of thing this summer.' And he put his
16 arms around me, and kissed my neck and said, 'You're not
17 everyone. You're my special girl. Do it just for me.' And he
18 was so sweet and gentle, I did it. Just to please him.

19   One time we were going somewhere. And just as we
20 were leaving, I remembered I had to phone a friend —
21 Irene — to make an arrangement with her. She wasn't at
22 home. She was at her boyfriend Jonathan's, so I called her
23 there, and he answered the phone. We spoke a little while,
24 then Irene came on the phone. I'd been out with Jonathan
25 a few times and Robert hated him and that whole crowd.
26 'Full of nonsense,' he said. 'They think they're a cut above
27 the rest of us.' When I got off the phone he was in such a
28 temper. 'Just get in the car,' he yelled and slammed the
29 door.

1   As he drove, he got more and more worked up. 'All I
2   hear these days is Jonathan Jonathan Jonathan,' he
3   screamed. I just sat there. I didn't know what to do, what
4   to say. He was being so unreasonable. Then he hit me. With
5   the back of his hand across the face. While he was driving.
6   I was so ... I'd never seen him like that before. I mean he'd
7   been jealous, but never like that. So I just sat there. I
8   didn't say a word. I was so shocked, and the tears began to
9   roll down my face. I couldn't stop them, and the more I
10   couldn't make them stop, the angrier I got. I was sobbing
11   and sobbing and I couldn't look at him ... I felt so ...
12   humiliated. And then he pulled the car over and stopped. I
13   turned to look at him — I wasn't sure what he was going to
14   do. He had tears in his eyes, he was crying himself. He said
15   he was sorry, would I forgive him, he'd never do it again. He
16   looked so pathetic. I believed him.
17
18
19
20
21
22
23
24
25
26
27
28
29
30
31
32
33
34
35

Nagasaki Dust
by W. Colin McKay

1 Kimiko — twenty   Female
2 Randolph — young man   Male
3
4 *(These two monologs are dramatic case studies that record the*
5 *horrific events of the atomic bomb destruction of Nagasaki,*
6 *Japan in World War II. Kimiko, a girl of twenty, weaves an*
7 *uneasy tapestry of her experience when she speaks of the death*
8 *of her infant child. Randolph, a young man whose father*
9 *survived the destructive holocaust, provides a more direct and*
10 *simple reaction to the devastation and its impact on his life.)*
11
12
13 **Kimiko:**
14 **I thought my baby would be safe with his Auntie. They told**
15 **me that Hiroshima had been destroyed. My whole family**
16 **was there. I had to go to them to see if they were safe, but**
17 **everyone was talking about strange things in the air that**
18 **killed you and made you sick. So I left Bontaro with Auntie**
19 **and took the train to Hiroshima. I didn't know what to**
20 **expect. All the talk seemed crazy. I mean, a town doesn't**
21 **just disappear. No bomb is that big. I prayed that my**
22 **family was safe. When I got to Hiroshima I knew they**
23 **weren't. The train rails stopped a few miles out of the city.**
24 **Just stopped. I had to walk the rest of the way into the**
25 **city. It was ... very hard. Where the city had been was a**
26 **place of the dead with burned corpses wherever I looked. I**
27 **never found my family. Where we had lived was nothing. I**
28 **cried all day and said prayers.**
29 **The next day I hurried back to my son, very early the**

1   morning of August ninth. That morning, Auntie had taken

2   Bontaro to Our Lady of the Immaculate Conception to pray

3   for the dead of Hiroshima, while I distributed the flyers John

4   had given me. *(The stage is suddenly dazzled with a blinding*

5   *LIGHT, then it's dark. There's the SOUND of a BOMB exploding,*

6   *then fading. After a moment, a solitary light comes up on Kimiko,*

7   *who stands, weeping.)* There had been five hundred people at

8   mass, praying, when the bomb was dropped. They all just

9   vanished. *(Pauses, then softly in anguish)* I didn't even wash

10   his blanket.

11

12   Randolph:

13   That last night at home before coming here, Dad and I

14   didn't stop arguing until the sun came up. I remember the

15   early light was just sneaking into the sky. We both were

16   looking out the window, watching it grow light ... quiet ...

17   exhausted ... thinking about how much we'd miss each

18   other and ... how much each other meant to us. We didn't

19   say so, but that's what we were thinking. It was an intimate

20   moment. Both of us getting to know each other a little

21   more. It was then I told him what I liked best about the law.

22   I hadn't told him before — mostly because I hadn't thought

23   of it until that moment. I believed ... really believed ... that

24   after careful legal analysis, almost every argument would

25   finally break down to an inevitable conclusion. I may not

26   have liked it, I may have ignored it. Hell, I may even have

27   denied it. But ... it'd be there. I told him that Midwest

28   concept, truly loved it — If you worked at something long

29   enough and hard enough, inevitably the truth would be

30   there. *(Falls silent, disturbed and almost angry)*

31   **Damn it.** *(Falls silent again. He stops, shakes his head in*

32   *resignation. There's a slight angry undertone to his voice)* The

33   key is to make sure your analysis has been complete and

34   thorough. *(Beat)* You see, there are three main ingredients to

35   any argument. The data ... *(Holds up one finger)* The warrant

1   ... *(Holds up a second finger)* ... which links the data to that
2   final, inevitable ... *(Holds up third finger)* conclusion. For
3   example, data — the airplane is on fire and is falling out of
4   the sky. Warrant — airplanes which are on fire and falling
5   out of the sky crash, usually killing everyone on board.
6   Conclusion — get the hell out of the plane, dummy. See?
7   Nothing to it. Except ... except if you've been performing
8   your analysis while urinating in the middle of a twister.

9   *(Hurriedly repeating himself)* Data — the airplane is on fire
10 and is falling out of the sky. Warrant — airplanes on fire and
11 falling out of the sky crash usually killing everyone on board.
12 *(Slows down)* But ... the army has ordered you to stay in the
13 plane until it crashes. So, if you follow orders, you'll die. On
14 the other hand, if you bail out, you'll get court-martialed and
15 shot. You die either way. Inevitable conclusion? You pee in
16 the middle of a twister, everybody gets wet.

17
18
19
20
21
22
23
24
25
26
27
28
29
30
31
32
33
34
35

The School Mascot
by A. C. Felicity Kozik

1   Amanda — teenager   Male/Female

2

3   *(Amanda, a naive but nimble high school student, provides an*

4   *intimate glimpse of the pleasure as well as the pain of being the*

5   *school mascot. There is a good blend of high spirits and high*

6   *jinks in this fun parody of adolescent days. Amanda's good-*

7   *natured account of embarrassing incidents is filled with the*

8   *despair most teenagers dread and teaches a delightful lesson.)*

9

10   Most people would think being that goof who dresses up as

11   the school mascot would be fun. Most schools have

12   mascots like Tigers, Vikings, Bears, Knights or Lions. I

13   wanted to get involved with that thing that they so

14   strangely titled 'school spirit.' I tried out, since last year's

15   mascot had moved to another school in Vienna. I was a

16   freshman, and like one I was determined to get the part. I

17   tried and the coach was saying, 'Are you sure, don't you

18   know ... ' I know all the details I told him. I figured it was

19   because I was a girl that he was so hesitant. How was I to

20   know my school's mascot was a giant sewer rat? After all

21   I hadn't been to any pep assemblies yet.

22   I get beat-up on a daily basis. First, because I am the

23   reject mascot, second because I'm also president of the

24   chess club, and third because I'm fifteen and still wear a

25   training bra. If I was head cheerleader I would receive

26   respect from my peers, even though sometimes some of

27   the most peppy cheerleaders have an I.Q. of fifty-seven. My

28   friends were supposed to keep my identity as the despised

29   mascot a secret, but instead they told the whole school.

1   I guess the reason I haven't quit yet is because of the
2   intimate relationship I hold with the guys varsity football
3   team. After the homecoming game the fullback and the
4   quarterback both gave me a present, a barrel of blue
5   gatorade over my head. One time the opposing school tried
6   to kidnap me, while in costume, as a practical joke. The
7   police finally found me, locked in an extra large dog carrier
8   on the side of the highway.
9   I guess I really should spend more energy on the chess
10   club. I win more matches than the two other members. By
11   day I'm your typical nerd, but by night I'm a giant sewer
12   rat! Next year I'm moving to Vienna for the same reason
13   last year's mascot did, a chance to change my identity. A
14   word of advice to any freshman of next year: school spirit
15   is actually something you'll find in creepy ghost stories.
16   Listen to me, or you may find your self parading around as
17   a giant sewer rat!
18
19
20
21
22
23
24
25
26
27
28
29
30
31
32
33
34
35

The Colour of Justice
by Richard Norton-Taylor

1 Neville Lawrence — adult	Male

2

3   *(This is a dramatic reconstruction of the 1999 public hearings*

4   *that erupted into national outrage in London, England when*

5   *black teenager Stephen Lawrence was stabbed to death by a*

6   *gang of white youths and the police investigation failed to*

7   *convict the alleged criminals. Now Neville Lawrence, Stephen's*

8   *father, talks about his son and the events leading up to the news*

9   *of his son's murder.)*

10

11   I was born on 13th March 1942 in Kingston, Jamaica. I

12   came to England in 1960 at the age of eighteen. When I

13   first came here I lived in Kentish Town, which at the time

14   was notorious for teddy boys and things like that. I was

15   available to work as an upholsterer because I had done my

16   apprenticeship and was therefore qualified. Unfortunately, I

17   was not able to get a job. I believe this was because of

18   racism ...

19   Stephen was born on September 13th 1974 at

20   Greenwich District Hospital. Stephen was very talented at

21   school. His favorite subject was art. One of the things we

22   discovered was that he wanted to be an architect; he was

23   very good at drawing. Stephen has never been in trouble.

24   We brought our children up to respect the law. On the

25   morning of April 22nd 1993 Stephen came into our

26   bedroom overlooking the road and said 'see ya later.' He

27   asked me if I was okay and I said, 'yes.' He went down and

28   returned upstairs and said, 'Are you sure you are all right,

29   Dad?' I said, 'yes.' Because I was not working I was not

1   feeling all that good about myself. I watched Stephen go
2   down the road with his rucksack over his back. That is the
3   last time I saw him alive.
4   At 10:30 p.m. there was a ring at the door bell. I
5   thought it was Stephen. It was Joey Shepherd. Joey told
6   me that Stephen had been attacked down the road at a bus
7   stop by the Welcome Inn Pub by about six white youths.
8   Doreen called the police who told her that they knew
9   nothing about the incident. I was just praying that he was
10   not dead. We just sat there. All sorts of things were going
11   through my mind. They came in the door. I do not
12   remember the exact words they used, but I do remember
13   they said that Stephen was dead, we could phone our
14   relatives or something like that ...
15   The next day is very cloudy. We still did not know how
16   Stephen had been killed. We were introduced to the two
17   liaison officers, D.S. Bevan and D.C. Holden. Holden made
18   a remark about woolen gloves and a hat being found. It was
19   clear she was implying that Stephen was a cat burglar.
20   There were incidents where our car tires were slashed. It
21   made us feel even more threatened. We had fears about
22   burying Stephen here because of the situation surrounding
23   his death. In June 1993, we flew to Jamaica with the body.
24   He is lying beside his grandmother in Clarendon in Jamaica.
25
26
27
28
29
30
31
32
33
34
35

Way Deep
by Katherine Wilcox Burger

1   Jolene — fifteen   Female

2

3   *(Two teenagers, Jolene and Tate, fall in love and decide to run*

4   *away from home. On the road, the first gush of love quickly sours*

5   *and they decide to return home. Jolene, who is fifteen, resembles*

6   *a sixteenth-century religious madonna — no, not the rock icon! But*

7   *she is also a fragile and vulnerable romantic, a good example of*

8   *the naive beauty and innocent wonder found in youth.)*

9

10   What I've heard is: there are only two stories in the whole

11   world. 'A stranger comes to town' and 'I go on a journey.'

12   Everything else — boy gets, loses, recovers girl; X betrays

13   Y over Z, Y stabs Z with a corkscrew — it's all variations

14   on the theme. Someone you know can turn out to be a

15   stranger, and the other way around. A journey can be

16   local. Not everyone has the wherewithal to travel. And

17   some journeys are inner, and I don't mean 'The Incredible

18   Voyage,' those medical rescue people bopping around in

19   some guy's bloodstream. Sometimes a person is exposed

20   to, I don't know, a new thought, a different perspective,

21   and it's as boggling as if they'd gone to outer space.

22   So here's the deal. In the summer of my fifteenth year

23   a stranger showed up in town and I ended up going on a

24   journey and then I went home again. In a nutshell. But it

25   was more complicated than that, at least to me. I guess I

26   should start at the beginning. He — the stranger — was

27   visiting his aunt Betsy because his parents were getting a

28   divorce and they wanted him out of the way. The first time

29   I saw him I felt like all the air in my chest just got

1   compressed, as if a hand was squeezing my heart. It didn't
2   get any better. It was, like, agony to see this guy. Not
3   seeing him was worse. I'd moon around and wear black a
4   lot, even though it was summer, and look in the mirror for
5   skin imperfections for hours. It's embarrassing to admit
6   how much time I spent looking in that mirror. Maybe I was
7   trying to go through the looking glass and find a backwards
8   world where I'd fit in more. And then one day he spoke to
9   me. I was nutzoid, gonzo, gone.
10   We started having these really deep conversations, not
11   a lot of gossip and hot air like the other kids. We talked
12   about important stuff. Big stuff. The eternal questions.
13   Death, life on other galaxies, is there a god or is life just a
14   panoply of chaotic happenstance.
15   I brought a blanket and some iced tea. I know what
16   you're thinking. Teenagers, a blanket, the stars — but it
17   wasn't like that. But then he touched me. He touched me
18   and the world was never the same again. And all above us
19   the stars were streaming, streaking through the black
20   night sky with a dying fall, like music too lovely to be
21   heard, too lovely to live.
22   I wanted to die. I figured that whatever else happened
23   during the whole rest of my life it would never be as good
24   as this. I wanted to die right now.
25
26
27
28
29
30
31
32
33
34
35

Jane: Abortion and the Underground
by Paula Kamen

1	Crystal — young woman	Female

2

3   *(In the early 1960s, a proactive women's rights group was*
4   *informally established in Chicago. The group, known only to a few*
5   *as "the Service," was to serve as a clearinghouse for information*
6   *and provide safe illegal abortions to women in desperate need.*
7   *Crystal, now a mature young woman, recalls her first encounter*
8   *with "the Service" while she was a sophomore in high school.)*

9

10   I was a sophomore in high school and I attended Rezin-Orr
11   High School on the West Side. It was located on Augusta
12   and Keeler. It's on Pulaski and Chicago Avenue now. One
13   of my high school chums came to me and told me that she
14   was pregnant, and she said she had to get an abortion. It
15   wasn't like thinking that maybe she should put it up for
16   adoption or what have you. She said that she had to get an
17   abortion. And I was a virgin, you know, so I was just
18   supportive. So I said, OK, I would support her. What
19   happened was she did all the contacting. I don't know how
20   she found the organization, but she came to school one day
21   and said, 'I found someone to give me an abortion — and I
22   have an appointment set up.'
23   So, I think that we even took public transportation to
24   this house ... And we went to this apartment and there was
25   a couple, a white couple and *(With some confusion)* ... I
26   believe it was the South Side.
27   Well, they started to describe what the procedure would

28

1   be like, but I'm sure the first thing they did was find out
2   how pregnant she was, what her age was, trying to
3   determine, you know, if she was a good candidate ... And
4   so I think we asked how much or something and they said
5   there's no set fee, but whatever you have. She had fifteen
6   dollars. I remember that. And so she gave them the money,
7   or however the arrangement, I don't know. *(Nods head)* ...
8   But I know she had fifteen dollars.
9   But we started crying at some point while she was
10   talking to us because we were so young. We asked if I
11   would be able to go with her, and that's when they told us
12   they had a place that I could go to while the procedure was
13   taking place.
14   Well, I remember her, too, you know, saying that in
15   terms of when it happened, that it was painful. You know,
16   that she cried and that whole thing because she went
17   through that alone ... I don't know if she ever told her
18   parents, but I know it was very traumatic, and it stayed
19   with me. I don't know how this woman could ever forget.
20
21
22
23
24
25
26
27
28
29
30
31
32
33
34
35

Eden Creek
by Dwight Watson

1 Abby — twenty-five   Female

2

3 *(Abby, a twenty-five-year-old honky-tonk woman, sits regally on*

4 *a barstool in a seedy backwoods lounge and talks to an*

5 *imaginary customer who sits at the table. She takes out a*

6 *compact to check her lipstick and begins to reflect on her life and*

7 *travels from a small rural town to the big, chilling city and then*

8 *back home again. Her quiet strength and fierce independence*

9 *lends a bittersweet quality to the long journey.)*

10

11 I left Eden Creek when I was sixteen. I couldn't bear the

12 thought of living in a small town any longer. It was dull.

13 Dull, honey, dull as dirt. Everybody knew everything you did

14 and what they didn't know they made up. Besides, I like

15 the night life, and the only night life you get in Eden Creek

16 takes the shape of barn swallows and bats. *(She fumbles*

17 *through her pocketbook looking for an ad from* Life *magazine.)*

18 I clipped this ad from *Life* magazine the day I left home.

19 Kept it near me ever since. Listen to what it says, 'Each week

20 the evidence becomes clearer that women like *Life*, subscribe

21 to *Life*, reserve copies, complain of shortage and want *Life*

22 just as men do, and for the same reasons.' I like the way it

23 keeps repeating Life, Life, Life, like Life is something bold and

24 important. *(She returns the ad to her pocketbook.)*

25 I was determined not to sit around and complain about

26 the shortage of life like every other dull person in Eden.

27 Like the man says, 'Some folks drinks to cut the fool, and

28 some folks drinks to think.' Well, I was sixteen and tired of

29 fools drunk from thinking about how depressing the

1   **Depression is.** *(Laughing)* **I subscribed to** *Life*! *(She crosses*
2   *behind the counter for a soft drink.)*
3   I began working in honky-tonks, well because they are
4   fun, lively and exciting. Every night I had a boy cuter than
5   the night before. Of course, most of the boys didn't have
6   money, not much, to spend. So, like all other honky-tonk
7   girls, I hooked me a fish, an automobile salesman. He was
8   much older than I was, but he was a lot of fun. There were
9   two things I didn't like about him though. One, his halitosis
10   or bad breath; and two, he wore flashy cheap suits. I could
11   get used to the cheap suits but, whew, that halitosis! I'd
12   get off work at three in the morning and he'd be waiting for
13   me fogging the windows with his halitosis. Since he worked
14   at a car lot, he could drive home a different car each night.
15   And since he was drunk most of the time, he'd let me
16   drive. I still get chills thinking about him laughing and me
17   in a new automobile each night tearing down the highway
18   fifty miles an hour. He called me 'Lucky' Teeter, you know,
19   after the crack daredevil driver from Noblesville. *(She crosses*
20   *from behind the counter and sits on a bar stool.)*
21   'Lucky' Teeter came to the Mooresville County Fair and
22   me and my girlfriend, Toni, went to see him. He was really
23   something. Wearing only a football helmet for protection,
24   he'd blow a kiss to his wife in the grandstand and then hop
25   in this brand new Plymouth. He'd circle the ramp two or
26   three times, building to a speed of forty-five, fifty-five, sixty-
27   five miles per hour, or better, and then he would hit the
28   ramp with only his left wheels, the car would turn over on
29   its side, slide for about 120 yards, flip up-right, and he'd
30   drive off. *(She rises.)* Can you believe that? It's the truth.
31   *(Crossing to the table.)*
32   I was told he made $50,000 a year for turning cars
33   over. Can you believe that? The next day Toni and I were
34   talking about the fame and fortune of 'Lucky' Teeter, and
35   we decided it was time to make a move to a bigger honky-

1   tonk in a bigger city. Like St. Louis. *(She sits at the table.)*
2   So, that night we found a man who said he was drunk
3   enough to drive us to St. Louis. But he sobered up a few
4   miles short of the state line and made us get out and walk.
5   He said the law would arrest him for violating the Mann Act
6   if he took girls across the state line. Toni said, 'Making a
7   girl get out and walk sounded like a man act to her.' Toni
8   was quick, and always saying something cute. He just
9   laughed, and said, 'I'm sorry but I can't afford trouble with
10   the law.' Well, we began hitchhiking and it wasn't long
11   before this real cute trucker picked us up. He said that it
12   was against company policy to pick up hitchhikers, but if
13   we didn't tell, he wouldn't. Well, we wouldn't tell! He was
14   driving one of those transport trucks hauling six or seven
15   new cars, some of them stacked on top of the others.
16   Sitting in the cab of his truck I could see the front bumper
17   of a car right there above me. I must have something for
18   men with new cars because in no time at all this driver had
19   talked me into taking an apartment with him. *(She rises and*
20   *crosses to the counter for her soft drink.)*
21   What I couldn't live with was him being gone all of the
22   time, so I started stepping out the nights he wasn't in. I told
23   you, I just love the night life. Well. I decided to throw a party
24   in the pink apartment one night when my trucker was away.
25   I'd been drinking and dancing with this fellow named
26   Darrick. Darrick was trying to convince me that there was
27   a pool table in my very own bedroom. I knew there wasn't
28   a pool table there, and I don't know what I was thinking, but
29   I went with him anyway. When we entered the bedroom I
30   said, 'See, there's no pool table here.' He just stood there
31   with this smile on his face. He had a real nice smile. Then
32   he said, 'We'd just have to use our imagination.' *(Slight*
33   *laugh.)* Well, we were beginning to use our imagination when
34   my trucker friend opens the bedroom door real sudden like.
35   'What the hell are you doing?' he said. First I thought I'd tell

1   him that Darrick was teaching me pool, but I knew the
2   trucker didn't have a sense of humor. So I said, 'If you
3 . don't know, I'm not going to tell you.'
4   Well, anyway. The trucker lacked imagination, so I left
5   him. I sure do miss that pink apartment though. *(Slight*
6   *pause.)* I went from one honky-tonk to another. I couldn't
7   find steady work. Most of my girlfriends, Toni and the rest,
8   were getting married, and then breaking up. I grew tired of
9   St. Louis. So, I moved back to Mooresville Pike, only
10   twenty miles from Eden. Been here ever since. *(She takes*
11   *the compact from her pocketbook and studies her face.)* I'm
12   better off here. Of course I can't save a nickel. In this
13   business you've got to look sharp. So I spend my money
14   buying clothes and keeping them clean. I get my hair done
15   once a week and keep my nails manicured. On a bad day I
16   even have to buy my own cigarettes and liquor. And then
17   there's Johnny, the boy I'm seeing now. He's just a farm
18   boy living near Eden Creek. I knew him in high school. He's
19   real sweet, but real poor. I buy him drinks now and then.
20   He says he wants to marry me. I keep putting him off. I
21   know his folks would be belching volcanoes if they thought
22   Johnny was going to marry me. What I mean is, I don't
23   think his folks could live with what I've done. *(Slight pause.*
24   *She puts the compact away.)*
25   I know I still have my form, but it's getting harder
26   attracting men when all they can think about is quail-breast.
27   You know, quail-breast, girls fifteen and sixteen years old.
28   Most of the quail-breast around here is pretty stupid. They
29   spend their time making it with schoolboys who don't have
30   nothing but looks. To make it in the honky-tonk you've got
31   to forget the schoolboys during working hours. *(Slight pause.)*
32   Johnny said that I'm going to make a good wife and mother.
33   Wife and mother! Imagine that! What would that do to my
34   form? *(She laughs.)* Johnny said that I was people wise. I'm
35   ignorant of the facts, but I know a lot about people. I've

listened daily to their personal histories. I've studied the geography of their worn and rugged faces. And when they leave me in the morning, or even after a few hours, or a few minutes, they have a new experience to think about, to reflect on. And I'm just a little, tiny bit smarter. I would marry Johnny if I could be sure he wouldn't be sorry later on, or if his folks could accept me. And even after I had lost my form, I wouldn't mind if he quail-breasted around a bit. As long as I didn't hear about it. As long as the quail wasn't in my bed. As long as he would come home to me. *(Slight pause.)* But you know how people talk. *(Enthusiastically.)* Let them! I subscribe to life! You sure you don't want something to drink?

'Off-Stage' Actors
by Ken Friedman

1   Unspecified   Male/Female
2
3   *(This collection of theatrical character sketches provides an off-*
4   *stage, intimate view of the frequent fits of despair experienced by*
5   *three unnamed stage performers. The monologs are compact and*
6   *rich in characterization that is suitable for male or female actors.*
7   *The three portraits offer a rare view of theatre performers as "people"*
8   *who voice their feelings with real-life honesty and sincerity.)*
9
10   First Actor:
11   I didn't know that Bobby was going to die. I should have
12   and I didn't. He had the disease. It was clear. I saw it on
13   his nose, that purple blotch. But, at that time, I was still
14   too stupid to make the connection. His friends, who knew,
15   made it a joke, because it was meant to be kept a secret.
16   We had been up in Boston doing a revival of a French play
17   and he was very good. He was very funny offstage and very
18   good on it. He was a better actor than I. When we got back
19   from Boston, I used to call him from time to time because
20   I liked him and I wanted to be his friend. As friendly and as
21   close as I can be, which is not that much. And, sometimes,
22   on the phone, he would answer with such terrible despair
23   in his voice. I would say, 'Hey, Bobby, is anything wrong?'
24   and he would say no and he would perk up, start doing his
25   routines and was funny. A couple of times we had dinner
26   together. He looked fine. He'd even made his hair blonde.
27   And then he disappeared. His friend said he was in North
28   Carolina taking care of his mother. But, he wasn't. He was
29   in a hospital, dying in New York. I'm glad I didn't know he

1   was dying. He was kind then, too. As an actor I may use
2   that shock, that disbelief and grief. That awful emptiness. I
3   may use it. But, I hope I never do. I hope I have enough
4   dignity to leave it where it belongs.
5
6   Second Actor:
7   I want to finish my comments by saying that a lot of the
8   success I've had in my brief Off-Broadway career I owe to my
9   training at this university and it's great to be back for a visit.
10 Any questions? Yes? Young lady? How do I warm-up? ... What
11 do you have in mind? Just kidding. You mean how do I
12 prepare prior to a particular performance? It's very simple. I
13 warm-up with the Ten Commandments. Oh, not all of them.
14 That would be ridiculous. Just a select few. Not for any
15 particular religious reason. I just like them. Now, I'm not
16 saying that this will work for you, but it does for me. No. I
17 don't want to do them now. Suffice to say I used to caw.
18 Caw! Caw! But, I started to sound like a bird. And I — Okay.
19 I'll do a few. My favorite warm-up Commandments.
20   Thou shalt not commit adultery! Thou shalt not commit
21 adultery. Ha! Ha! Thou shalt not commit adultery! Ha! Thou
22 shalt not covet thy neighbor's wife! Thou shalt not covet thy
23 neighbor's wife. Oh, yeah. Oh, yeah ... Thou ... well, you get
24 the drift. It frees me. Oh, by the way, I may be doing a film
25 with Dustin Hoffman, Gene Hackman and Gregory Peck, but
26 it's too soon to talk about. Any other questions? How much
27 money did I make last year? Well, I don't like to brag about
28 those things. But, in the solid six figures ... unfortunately, that
29 includes cents. Listen, I don't want to give you the impression
30 that I'm a huge success, but I'm working and I have made
31 some big contacts with very important people. Questions?
32 No, the last movie was not soft porn. One of those is enough.
33 Well, let me finish by saying just a few years ago, guys, I was
34 sitting where you are and now, look at me. Remember: work
35 hard, don't despair, and meet people who can further your

1 career. Oh, this afternoon, I'll be over in the cafeteria,
2 hanging out, so if any of you want to come over and talk
3 some more, particularly the girls, just kidding, just kidding,
4 feel free. So, it's great to be back where it all started and
5 thank you very much.
6
7 Third Actor:
8 Today, I had my third rejection this month. But, who
9 cares? Because, I will make it. I was turned down for a role
10 in a revival of *Equus*. A fine show. I was too old for the kid,
11 too young for the psychiatrist, and too small for the horse.
12 But I went anyway, and I was turned down. But, I will make
13 it. Last week I auditioned for a ten-city tour of *The Pajama*
14 *Game*. I can sort of sing. I can't dance. I wasn't right for
15 any of the roles — but what the hell, I went anyway. I will
16 make it. A month ago I was up for *Summer and Smoke*. I
17 was perfect for that. I can play any of the roles. You know
18 that. I gave a fabulous audition. Nothing. But, I am not
19 discouraged. I'm not saying that I'm encouraged, either.
20 But I did give two great auditions and I will make it. I will
21 make it. I have a lot of talent. Everyone who's seen my
22 work knows that. I have ability. I will make it. I will make
23 it! I WILL make it. I WILL make it! I WILL make it! I am
24 hungry. AND I WILL MAKE IT! OH GOD, LET ME MAKE
25 IT! I WILL MAKE IT! I WILL MAKE IT! I MUST MAKE IT! I
26 WILL ... MAKE IT! ... and if I don't? So what. I'm not going
27 to let it bother me.
28
29
30
31
32
33
34
35

Under Siege
by G. L. Horton

1   Ruth — young woman   Female

2

3   *(Ruth, a young woman who was raped by her girlfriend's*

4   *husband, confides in a sympathetic counselor at an abortion*

5   *clinic. She confronts the anger and bitterness of the physical*

6   *violation with courage and is able to tell the counselor what she*

7   *would never tell her family or friends. Ruth's searing pain emerges*

8   *with quiet dignity as she recalls the brief and brutal incident.)*

9

10   The three of us were watching T.V. when my girlfriend

11   decided to go out and get us a pizza. While she was gone,

12   her husband raped me. I couldn't believe it was happening.

13   It was so fast. Before this he'd never even made a pass.

14   When he got off me, I ran and locked myself in the

15   bathroom. I was sick in the toilet, twice, and then I took a

16   shower. When I heard my girlfriend come home, I came out,

17   and there they were, the two of them, eating pizza. He was

18   eating and talking and laughing and acting friendly, like it

19   was nothing.

20   I told Linette I was sick and I was going home. And I

21   haven't been over there since. We used to get together all

22   the time. So now my girlfriend's beginning to wonder. She

23   asks me, 'Ruth, is anything wrong?' But I can't tell her.

24   She thinks they're happy. She thinks he loves her.

25

26

27

28

29

Up, Up and Away!
by Ludmilla Bollow

1   Unspecified — sixteen   Female

2

3   *(A good-humored young girl, eyes tightly closed and hands*
4   *clenched, has a sky-high "sweet sixteen" birthday celebration on a*
5   *hot air balloon! At first, the young girl is anxious and hesitant, but*
6   *soon she is soaring at ease toward the heavens. This warm-spirited,*
7   *high-flying adventure sparkles with glints of genuine tenderness and*
8   *suggests there may be more here than mere surface appearances.)*

9

10   Ooooh — ooooh! My stomach's turning somersaults! I'm
11   afraid to open my eyes. I have no idea where I am ... Why
12   did I ever even think I wanted to do this! I musta been crazy
13   — telling my friends — that this was my total dream wish.
14   Hey, I'm even afraid to go up in a ferris wheel — all those
15   sky ride kinda things. What made me think going up in a
16   hot air balloon would be something to wish for.
17   Okaay — I'm going to open my eyes now — and stop
18   concentrating on my queasy stomach. Slowly, one eye at a
19   time. *(Huge breath)* Oh my god! We're already so high up.
20   Steady now. Deep breath. Absorb it all. *(Pause)*
21   Clouds — I can almost reach out and touch them. What
22   a fantastic view! Everywhere! We're not rising any higher
23   now — kinda just sailing along — like on this huge ocean
24   of air. My stomach's settling too. Maybe, just maybe it
25   could turn into a beautiful day — my sixteenth birthday. My
26   friends, such a super group of girls — they did this for me
27   — my big, big surprise! They remembered me once saying,
28   as I looked up into the sky punctuated with colorful
29   balloons, me shouting out, 'I'd give anything to go up in

1 one of those space ships, just once in my lifetime! My
2 biggest wish ever!' They yelled back, 'You hate flying, abhor
3 ferris wheels.' 'But,' I said, 'a balloon's different — you just
4 soar above the world. Like when I sometimes dream I'm
5 flying, floating above the earth. What fun to experience
6 while I'm wide awake.'

7 I thought they forgot about it. Then, this morning, they
8 literally kidnapped me, wouldn't tell me where we were
9 going. And when the blindfold came off — here I was, right
10 smack in this hot air balloon field. Big sign — 'One Hour
11 Rides — All Day Long!'

12 'Your Sweet Sixteen Birthday Present!' they yelled. All
13 of a sudden I got panicky. I didn't really want to go up in
14 one of those strange looking monsters. It had all been a
15 fantasy thing, not something I really wanted to happen. But
16 I couldn't tell them — too late. No matter, I'd have to lie,
17 say I loved it and all that other garbage — if I lived through
18 it — if we got back down to earth okay. 'Be careful what you
19 wish for —' the meaning suddenly became clear.

20 Okay, I'm going over the edge now, so I can look over
21 and down. One step at a time. Just me, the navigator, and
22 two other people in this basket. A couple in love. You can
23 tell, they're clinging so tight to each other, joyous looks on
24 their faces, as if they were floating off to heaven. Whew, I
25 made it! At the edge. Hang on tight. Grip that rail. Looking
26 down now. Ooooh — it'sooo faaar down. Look! There's the
27 girl gang, waving and shouting, looking like joyous little
28 bugs. Oh, oh, we're moving away, faster now — .

29 Somewhere down there's my house — my school —
30 Know what — it's kinda beautiful up here! I feel almost like
31 an angel, flying above everybody, watching over them. I
32 don't have a care in the world right now. Free as a bird. This
33 is how birds must feel as they skim across the skies. What
34 a wonderful trip, and I still have forty-five minutes to go! I
35 can't wait to tell my friends that this was the best present

1 ever. My sixteenth birthday — the day I sailed up and over
2 the rainbow ...
3
4
5
6
7
8
9
10
11
12
13
14
15
16
17
18
19
20
21
22
23
24
25
26
27
28
29
30
31
32
33
34
35

Beach Music
by Rick Doble

1 Unspecified — elderly   Female
2
3   *(An older, single woman lies in bed late at night and listens to*
4   *the hypnotic, pulsating sounds coming from the rented room of*
5   *her boarders. She is a forlorn, solitary figure who has weathered*
6   *a cruel and harsh life. Surrounded by dusty artifacts and relics*
7   *of the past, the unnamed woman cautiously spins a cynical tale*
8   *of human frailty before she slips into a final, restful sleep.)*
9
10   Usually, I can sleep like a stone. Lightning seeking the
11   ground next to my bedroom, or birds calling loudly in the
12   morning, have never bothered me. So why am I listening to
13   the slight whine of box springs in the room I rented? My
14   boarders are softly rocking. Through the plaster walls I
15   hear their breathing, his sudden puff of air. Then the
16   springs ebb to silence, and what's left is the rhythm of their
17   snores. But still I cannot sleep.
18   I came to St. Augustine to find a husband. And after
19   two years, all I've got is three jobs and a hundred dancing
20   shoes. Twice a week I instruct retired men in the art of
21   shagging. It's the one job that I really enjoy. And they flirt
22   with me, always ask me to marry them, maybe a little
23   seriously at times. We laugh and even pretend that I will,
24   until it's ten o'clock. Then we close for the night. They're
25   nice, these older men. They think I'm beautiful and treat
26   me with respect. Although, I admit, on bad days I giggle
27   only to keep them coming back. On those nights, I feel
28   heavy, clumsy. Their touch and smell make my skin crawl.
29   But I smile and snuggle into their shoulders anyway. Next

1 time, when I'm in a better mood, I may want them, so I
2 chose not to spoil things.
3   My day job at the university is full of paper and
4 procedure, and I often long for another's touch. So on good
5 evenings I kick off my shoes and dance barefoot with all the
6 men who have come just for me. And later when I lie here,
7 I can feel each of their wrinkled hands on my waist, my
8 shoulder, the weight and pull of their flesh. It's like having
9 ridden a car for hours, responding to its motion even after
10 it's come to rest. And then I think of my high school
11 boyfriend, gentle, quiet, angry, who took me swimming in
12 the cool rivers of the Georgia foothills. My first lover, a
13 married man, who held me so carefully I felt like a bowl he
14 was afraid to spill. And my fiance whose touch felt like
15 flower petals, until he scraped my skin like rose stems, and
16 our wedding plans ended. But of course who I really want
17 is my husband. I've always believed that one day I'd find
18 'him,' and he would fully hold me, envelop me like no one
19 ever has, make me whole. Still, where he is, is a mystery.
20   I am the oldest of a family of five children and none of
21 us has married or stayed married. My parents' relationship
22 was strained at best. As kids we ran between the vacant
23 rooms of their boarding house, while my mother changed
24 the sheets, swept the remains of the night before into a
25 waste paper basket. Guests liked us because she would
26 never tell what she heard or saw. The house became a
27 game of hide-and-seek between the wishes of Mom and
28 Dad, each of us learning how to play their contradictions to
29 our advantage. I guess I sided with Father. Mother seemed
30 so cold. Dad was ineffectual and moralistic, but always had
31 time for me, made me feel I was his 'girl.'
32   I reach for a glass of water on my window sill when a
33 flash of lightning illuminates my room. The walls, my oak
34 bureau, the pictures of my family are now bathed in a steel
35 blue light. I sit up and look down on the outside just as

1   another vein cuts across the sky. It glows on the tree tops,
2   the shiny lawns below. Dark rain like a curtain follows,
3   tapping on my glass. And then the voice begins to fade, the
4   one that's been keeping me awake. I slide back beneath my
5   soft covers, feel as though I'm floating. Now ... at last I can
6   feel sleep near me. It's coming closer, over taking me. It
7   wraps itself around me ... I fall into its stream.
8
9
10
11
12
13
14
15
16
17
18
19
20
21
22
23
24
25
26
27
28
29
30
31
32
33
34
35

Two Mens'es Daughter
by J. e. Franklin

1   Goldie — age unspecified   Female
2
3   *(Goldie, an African-American woman, is tortured by childhood*
4   *memories. The recent death of Old Cecil-Morrow, her white father,*
5   *only adds to the complications of her troubled life. Weeping quietly*
6   *in a dimly-lit room, Goldie speaks softly to her niece, Addie, and*
7   *tells the sobering story of why she sits in the darkness. There is a*
8   *sense of urgency in her voice as she reveals her troubled past.)*
9
10   Mama wasn't nothing but a kid when she went to work for
11   him. Everywhere she turned, there he was, even after
12   Daddy Randall married her. Ain't many Colored men wants
13   a Colored woman got white men's chill'un, but Daddy
14   Randall loved us just like we was his'n. Old Cecil-Morrow
15   wanted to get even, cheated him out-a some money, mad
16   cause he married mama. What could a Colored man do
17   back then? He didn't have no rights a white man was
18   bound to respect. I hadn't even quit peeing-the-bed yet the
19   first time I cussed him. I didn't know what I was saying.
20   Just repeating words I'd heard the grown-folks use. He told
21   mama to beat me but she wouldn't. That let me know I
22   could keep it up, even after he told me he was my daddy.
23   I told him, 'You might-a been the one sired me, but you
24   ain't my daddy. If I pass on the road and see you laying in
25   a gully dying, I'll pass on by like I don't even know you and
26   let you die.' Me being the baby, I could get away with
27   anything, even after I got grown. Tootie and Cecil-David
28   thought he'd sic the Klu-Kluk-Klan on me, but he didn't. I
29   didn't care. Something had a-holt'a me. Mama'd say, real

1   quiet, 'Don't do evil for evil, baby. When somebody do you
2   evil, do 'em good.' But I knowed her heart ... Or thought I
3   did. 'Til one day she told me I had ways just like him. I'm
4   shamed to even repeat what I said to my mama. I know I
5   hurt her to her heart cause she just left me to God then.
6   The Bible tell you not to cuss your mama ... and your daddy
7   ... or your lamp be put out in everlasting darkness. That's
8   why I stays in this room. Guess I'm just waiting for the lamp
9   to go out ... cause God don't like ugly. He just don't!
10
11
12
13
14
15
16
17
18
19
20
21
22
23
24
25
26
27
28
29
30
31
32
33
34
35

Please Hear What I'm Not Saying
by Anonymous

1	Unspecified

Male/Female

2

3   *(Here is the first of two brief audition "companion pieces" useful*
4   *to satisfy a shorter one- or two-minute audition time limit.*
5   *Written as a diary entry, the first companion piece uses the*
6   *image of a mask to remind us that "disguise" is simply a*
7   *recognition of our urgent need to regain a sense of personal,*
8   *individual identity. There is a measure of irony in the final lines*
9   *that needs distinct pausing and phrasing for emphasis.)*

10

11   Don't be fooled by me.
12   Don't be fooled by the face I wear.
13   For I wear a mask. I wear a thousand masks,
14   Masks that I'm afraid to take off,
15   And none of them are me.
16   I give the impression that I'm secure,
17   That all is sunny and unruffled with me,
18   Within as well as without.
19   But don't believe me, please?
20   I'm afraid that deep-down I'm nothing,
21   That I'm just no good, and that you
22   Will see this and reject me.
23   So I play my game, my desperate
24   Pretending game. With a facade of
25   Assurance without, and a trembling
26   Child within. And so begins the
27   Parade of masks, the glittering
28   But empty parade of masks.
29   Who am I, you may wonder?

1	I am someone you know very well.
2	For I am every man you meet, and
3	I am every woman you meet.
4	
5	
6	
7	
8	
9	
10	
11	
12	
13	
14	
15	
16	
17	
18	
19	
20	
21	
22	
23	
24	
25	
26	
27	
28	
29	
30	
31	
32	
33	
34	
35	

Groaning Up
by Jim Chevallier

1 Unspecified	Male/Female

2

3   *(The second "companion piece" is another brief but entertaining*
4   *script that asks the ultimate philosophical question, "What's so*
5   *great about growing up?" The character has an amusing point of*
6   *view and offers an ingenious response to the age-old question.*
7   *There is a comic tone in the proposal, but the serious elements*
8   *of doubt and despair emerge in the unnamed character's tirade.)*

9

10   So, what's so great about growing up?

11   The way it looks to me, everything slows down. It's like
12   they put you in this harness and then they make you pull
13   and the next thing you know you're an ox — big and heavy
14   and slow. And dull. That's the worst part. You look at
15   people over thirty and you know exactly how they're going
16   to be. They've got their job and they've got their ideas and
17   maybe they're married and so they've got that too. And
18   they just get into their groove and they start walking it, you
19   know. They just keep going round-and-round in it until it
20   becomes this rut. And after a while, it gets so deep that
21   the best they can do is not sink in it. Sink until they
22   disappear.

23   So what I'm saying is, what's the point? Why would you
24   want to end up like that, when you can be young and take
25   chances and have ideas? You know, while you still can be
26   somebody? Have a life. Why would you want to do that,
27   huh? Why would you want to just like give up?

28   It's not like you don't have a choice.

29

Happy Hour
by John J. Wooten

1 Frank — age unspecified   Male
2
3 *(Frank, a father with a spirit of recklessness, owns a small bar*
4 *in a sleepy town. He and his son, Jack, share a number of dark,*
5 *haunting secrets that drive them to senseless verbal abuse. After*
6 *an increasingly angry confrontation, Frank reveals to his son that*
7 *he allowed his daughter, Kate, to dance at his bar. There is a*
8 *hint of danger lurking in the air as Frank admits the long kept*
9 *secret to Jack.)*
10
11 It was supposed to be for one night ... We were out of
12 money. The savings. Your mother's trust. All of it. Gone.
13 But I had a big group coming in. Big. Enough to keep us
14 afloat for awhile. Then Gabrilla quits on me. Walks right in
15 and quits. Just like that. I ... I thought that was it. I was
16 ready to let the Sands go. Close her down. *(Lowers himself*
17 *into a chair)* But your sister wouldn't let me. Said she
18 couldn't stand to see me lose the place ... They loved her.
19 Bunch of college boys. Harmless. It was easy. Too easy.
20 She danced twice and waited in the office until they left. We
21 made a lot of money that night. Most we ever had. I told
22 her that was it but she wanted to do one more night. Just
23 until I found another girl. Said it didn't bother her.
24   Well, one night turned into two and two turned into a
25 week. I hired another girl but business fell off. So Kate
26 insisted on dancing again. At least until we got out of the
27 hole. Then she started hanging out with some of the
28 regulars. Between sets. I couldn't take it. I told her she had
29 to stop. She wouldn't so I made her stop. Business

1   dropped off again but I didn't care. I tried putting her back

2   behind the bar but that's when she met up with Tate. I told

3   her she would have to spend nights in the trailer with you,

4   that I didn't want her in the bar anymore. That's when she

5   left. Moved in with him ... It ... *(Frank looks at Jack for the*

6   *first time in the speech)*

7   It was only supposed to be a temporary thing, Jack. To

8   get some business in here. I never expected that they

9   would come just to see her ... that she'd want them to

10   come. Once I saw what was happening I knew I had to stop

11   it and I did. I did, Jack. If I could take it all back, I would.

12   I'd burn this damn place down to take it back. I swear to

13   God I would.

14

15

16

17

18

19

20

21

22

23

24

25

26

27

28

29

30

31

32

33

34

35

Leftovers
by Rodney James Scott

1	David — young man

Male

2

3   *(David, a free-spirited, inquisitive young man enjoys taking a*
4   *routine shortcut through the city cemetery. He soon finds himself*
5   *in a one-sided relationship with the "tenants" of the deceased*
6   *community. There is an initial detachment in David's gloomy*
7   *graveyard observations, but he also provides an intimate glimpse*
8   *of his own human frailty and inevitable mortality as well.)*

9

10   I walk this way all the time, I mean, it's shorter than going
11   all the way around. Sometimes I follow the paths, and other
12   times, if I am in a hurry or something, I just make a bee-
13   line straight across. It's more peaceful than on the streets,
14   real quiet, except for birds, or squirrels, or maybe an
15   airplane flying overhead. I like it. Some people are afraid of
16   the graveyard, but not me.

17   If you think about it, it could really get to you, at least
18   it does to some people, but not me. There are bodies down
19   there, just a few feet under the grass. I like to think of
20   them as leftovers, like when life is over, that is what there
21   is left. They are down there, out of sight, but still there. I
22   often wonder what they look like, how they died, and who
23   loves them. How great it would be if you could see into their
24   lives. They all lived, they did things, they had friends,
25   husbands, lovers, children. Some of them had great
26   adventures, went places, did extraordinary things, but now,
27   they are all the same, just leftovers.

28   I could always tell the well-to-do. They have big heavy
29   headstones, or above-ground vaults, but nearly always

1   plastic flowers. Some even have little fences around their
2   lot, like they are still trying to tell the world something. My
3   favorite graves have little stones, sometimes almost
4   overgrown with cemetery grass, and little cans with
5   daffodils, or pansies, or maybe dandelion. These leftovers
6   have people who love them still.
7   　　I read the dates. Born, July 9, 1942, Died December
8   21, 1948. She died at six years old. What could have
9   happened to a six year old that she would be here so early?
10   Was it disease, or an accident? What did she look like?
11   What does she look like now? I guess I could probably find
12   out some of the answers if I really wanted to, like go back
13   through the newspapers, or try to find relatives. I prefer not
14   to, I prefer to let them rest.
15   　　In some ways I think it is almost wrong to treat the
16   dead like we do. We fill the bodies with preservative, lay
17   them in air-tight coffins, and seal them in concrete vaults.
18   It seems like maybe we keep them from doing what is
19   natural, returning to the mother earth. Maybe that's where
20   they belong, once more at peace, at total rest, at one with
21   the elements from which their bodies were composed.
22   　　Within a few months of walking this way, I began to
23   develop relationships, certainly one-sided, but an
24   acknowledgement of their existence there below the grass.
25   Sally Mayfield, Born September 23, 1954, Died January 11,
26   1977. I talk to Sally quite a bit, mostly just in passing, like
27   'It's a nice day today Sally,' or 'How are you today Sally,'
28   just something like that. But sometimes it is more. She
29   was twenty-three, twenty-three years old, and laid to rest.
30   It's a little bit sad, even now. Life is so wonderful when you
31   are twenty-three. I would like to know what she looked like,
32   and hear replies from my words of greeting. I think I like
33   Sally. We were born the same year.
34   　　That's the way life is, do you know what I mean? You
35   just never know what is going to happen, or when it is

233

1   going to be over. You are born, and then you die, it's really
2   that simple. Some people just die earlier.

3   I thought once that I would like to dig her up, not like a
4   robber, or some kind of a pervert or anything, but just so
5   we could have a face-to-face conversation. I know she
6   wouldn't be looking her best, but friends don't worry about
7   such things, friends appreciate you for who you really are.
8   It would be much better than the casual 'How are you today
9   Sally,' that must do for now. There are many here who I
10   would have liked to know. Many of them have been here
11   since before I was born, but in mother earth, all are made
12   equal. Time is not an issue.

13   I have purchased a lot of my own, it's in a new section
14   of the cemetery. They have planted a few trees, but they are
15   too small to give any shade yet. I would have liked to get a
16   lot closer to Sally, but they were all inhabited. Someday I
17   will be here, just a few feet below the grass, resting in
18   peace until ... I hope someone will say 'Hello' every now and
19   then, and read the name and dates of my passing, and
20   know that I was here. I lived, and I loved, and I went the way
21   of all men. And by the way, dandelions would be just fine.
22   I love dandelions.

23
24
25
26
27
28
29
30
31
32
33
34
35

Typical Day
by Jonathan Walton

1 Unspecified — adult   Male

2

3   *(An innocent man has spent eight years in prison and is*
4   *scheduled to be executed today. Sitting alone in a small,*
5   *concrete cell on death row, the man confronts a grim reality.*
6   *Anxiety and fear are constant companions here as the man*
7   *reflects on the tragic events that have led to this final waiting*
8   *place. His personal chronicle is a gut-wrenching, unsettling*
9   *testimony that raises basic questions about our own humanity.)*

10

11   For eight long years I have sat upon death row and finally
12   the day has come that my curtain is going to close. For 243
13   months, I have been locked inside this cell and for 2920
14   days my life has been nothing short of hell. The moment
15   draws near where I will take my last walk *(Pause)* and with
16   the victim's family I will have my very last talk. As I finish
17   the last bite of this, my last meal, the concept of death I
18   begin to grasp. To a wooden chair my body will be
19   strapped, and a metal cap put upon my head — electricity
20   will be run throughout my entire body until at last, I am
21   dead. Ten pairs of eyes will stare, gape, and gawk, quite
22   possibly enjoying the sight of my life being lost.
23   I remember staring into those same eyes, those same
24   frowning faces. The prosecutor shouting insults, back and
25   forth as he paces. I testified in my own defense, 'I wasn't
26   there,' I cried. 'I don't even own a gun, so how in God's
27   name could I have shot someone?' Upon the truth I swore
28   and all of the words I said were true but all at once the
29   lawyer turned and said, 'Why should they believe you?' The

1   foreman began to rise and he handed down a verdict of
2   guilty. All at once I rose to my feet and at the top of my
3   lungs, I began to scream, 'I don't belong in prison — get
4   your hands off of me!' I fought as they put cuffs on my
5   hands, and chains on my feet. But it didn't matter what I
6   did — to prison they carried me. My lawyer filed appeal
7   after appeal, but we could make no one believe. Awaiting
8   my sentence, I sat within this cement block. I spent many
9   nights crying out to God, 'Lord I have done nothing wrong,
10   nothing! Please God, don't leave me here to rot. I don't
11   think I could take it Lord. No, I know that I could not.' Later
12   that month I received my sentence. The words pierce my
13   heart to this day. The foreman again stood to rise and
14   before he sat, I was condemned to die.
15   I haven't seen the stars in eight years. If you could
16   count the drops in the oceans — only then could you begin
17   to count my tears. I am all but forgotten. My family no
18   longer visits me. All I have left are thoughts and memories.
19   My mother used to cook breakfast on Sunday morning as
20   she sang "Amazing Grace" — the love of God shown off her
21   face. As she kneaded biscuits it would go something like
22   this ... *(Sings verse of "Amazing Grace.")* My wife, she had the
23   smile of an angel. I swear you could see wings if you gazed
24   from just the right angle. The birth of my daughter, so
25   small within my arms. I remember the first time she called
26   me Daddy, it filled a void within my heart.
27   But my third year here, my momma passed away. I
28   missed her funeral, the month of January, that fourth
29   Monday. My wife remarried and my daughter should be
30   thirteen. I am all but forgotten, no more visits to Daddy.
31   The last bite settles in my stomach and the warden
32   instructs me to rise. I have resolved in my mind that I am
33   going to die. I walk the last hundred feet, one foot in front
34   of the other — left then right, left then right. The chains
35   clank across the floor. I squint my eyes in the light. I try to

1 turn my wrists but I meet pain — the shackles so tight. I
2 walk into the room, with my head held high. I enter the
3 witnesses' midst wearing not a frown but a smile. The
4 executioner asked for my last words and I look each victim
5 in the eyes.

6 'The state killed me years ago, gave me a number. I no
7 longer had a name. Inmate number 49536. I was not a
8 person. I was a convict. I used to be a man until I came
9 here. Now I'm part of an unwanted clan. A group of
10 rejected individuals, clasped in chains and wearing orange
11 suits. This was not the way it was supposed to be! Just as
12 your loved one's life was stolen, the state, the judge, the
13 jury — each and every one of you stole my life from me. I
14 have been raped and beaten, ridiculed and scorned. I
15 looked up to God and cursed the day I was born. My spirit
16 is broken and my heart forever dismayed. My body stands
17 before you, but my mind has passed away.'

18 The shackles were secure and the metal cap put into
19 place as the tears began to flow down my troubled face.
20 'Please Lord, take me quick! I am not worthy of this
21 punishment. You are the only one who can read my heart and
22 you know that I am innocent.' I looked over to the wall and
23 the executioner began to reach for the lever. So before the
24 electricity flowed through my veins, I look up to heaven. 'The
25 Lord is my Shepherd, I shall not want. He maketh me to lie
26 down in green pastures, He leadeth me beside still waters.
27 He restoreth my soul. He leadeth me on the path of
28 righteousness for his namesake. Yea, though I walk through
29 the valley of the shadow of death; I will fear no evil, for Thou
30 art with me.' *(Stops abruptly, body convulses, and dies.)*

31
32
33
34
35

Love Is a Place
by Robin Glasser

1 Emma — fifteen   Female

2

3   *(Emma, a passionate young woman experiencing the first pangs*

4   *of innocent love, now struggles to understand the sudden and*

5   *unexpected suicide of her boyfriend, Jack. Her personal crisis is*

6   *heightened by a chilling fear that gives rise to Emma's own*

7   *suicide wish to join Jack. The unsettling horror that follows offers*

8   *a grim reminder of the fateful cost of shattered youthful dreams.)*

9

10   They laughed. They all laughed at me. All of my supposed

11   friends laughed at me! I can't believe that I really thought

12   they were my friends! Jack, they laughed at me when I

13   cried because the cafeteria reminded me of you. That was

14   where we first kissed. Do you remember? Of course you

15   don't remember. You can't remember. You're dead! Why did

16   you have to leave me? I need you. Nobody understands,

17   Jack. They all think that I'm just being melodramatic.

18   They all say that just because we're 15 that it couldn't

19   have been love. But it was love! I loved you then, and I love

20   you now. Why'd you do it? Whatever it was, you could've

21   talked to me about it. We would have worked something

22   out. That note that you left behind didn't do much to

23   console me.

24   'Dear Emma: I love you, but there are some things that

25   even love can't conquer. I have problems that you couldn't

26   even imagine, and I don't want to get you involved. This

27   has nothing to do with you. Please don't blame yourself.

28   Even if you were here, there's nothing that you could do to

29   stop me. My mind's made up. I know what I have to do. I'll

1   always love you. Love, Jack.'

2   Even if you were here there's nothing that you could do

3   to stop me? What do you mean there's nothing that I

4   could've done? I know that if I had been there things would

5   have turned out differently. Jack, my heart is breaking. You

6   made me realize that I was special. You showed me that I

7   do matter, and when you needed me to be there for you, I

8   wasn't there. Everything that happened in my life before I

9   met you is meaningless, as is everything that has

10   happened since your suicide. It makes me so angry that no

11   one thinks that it's possible to be in love just because of

12   our age. Is age really what matters? Are they saying that if

13   soul mates meet before they are 21, then it won't be love?

14   How old do you have to be for love to be real? I don't care

15   what they think about our relationship. It was real. I know

16   it, and you know it, and that's all that matters.

17   I miss everything about you. You can't imagine how

18   difficult it is being here without you. My best friend in the

19   whole world, the one person that I could tell anything to, is

20   gone. Gone forever. I always thought that we would grow

21   up, get married, have kids, become grandparents, and

22   grow old together. But now that'll never happen. You know

23   the saying, you always hurt the ones you love? Well, I see

24   just how true it is now. I know that you loved me despite

25   all of my flaws, yet still you hurt me in the worst way

26   possible. You left. When you were here, I felt like I belonged

27   to the world. Now that you're gone, I'm a lonely soul

28   floating aimlessly throughout the world. You were my guide

29   on the path of life, and without you I'm lost.

30   Jack, I can't deal with this anymore. I know that it's

31   only been about a month, and everyone says that it will get

32   easier, but I know that although that may apply to others

33   in similar situations, it doesn't apply to me. This will never

34   get any easier. It will only get harder, as the days pass and

35   the realization that you're gone forever sets in on me. I

1   have no one here to help me deal with this. You were the
2   only one who understood me. My love for you was what kept
3   me going, but it's getting harder with everyone saying that
4   it wasn't really love. I know that it was love. That love kept
5   me going, and now, in the end, it's also what's tearing me
6   apart. I suppose that you could say that it's almost like a
7   drug. Love, that is. I was down when we met, and your love
8   helped me to get out of my rut and up into the clouds.

9   I can't live without your love, so it's now clear what I
10   have to do. Juliet said to Romeo, 'and all my fortunes at thy
11   foot I'll lay, and follow thee my lord throughout the world.'
12   Now it's my turn to follow you throughout the world or after
13   world. I don't care where we are as long as we're together,
14   and the only way that we can be together is in death. In
15   your note you said that there was nothing that I could do to
16   stop you. Now, there's nothing that you can do to stop me.
17   I'm coming to join you, Jack! *(Emma opens a nearby window*
18   *that's on the 4th floor.)*

19   They say that it is better to have loved and lost than to
20   never have loved at all. I think that whoever said that is the
21   wisest man who ever lived. I'm going to make up my own
22   saying now. Love is the place where two perfectly
23   harmonious souls meet and live. In that place, nothing
24   matters. Not age, race, religion or anything. That, Jack, is
25   where I met you. *(Emma puts her feet through the window,*
26   *then the rest of her body. Takes one look inside, and jumps.)*

27

28

29

30

31

32

33

34

35

Rememberin' Stuff
by Eleanor Harder

1   Tony — adolescent   Male

2

3   *(Tony, a rebellious young man with an attitude, sits impatiently*

4   *in a group therapy session waiting for his turn to speak. He is a*

5   *troubled adolescent, consumed by frequent outbursts of anger*

6   *and an uncontrollable dependency on alcohol. When the*

7   *brooding Tony begins "rememberin' stuff," we catch a more*

8   *personal glimpse of his searing pain and suffering.)*

9

10   Yeah, I share an interest. *(To audience)* **Share it with a lot of**

11   **people. Alcohol. So, okay, what's that got to do with the**

12   **price of beans? Well, 'cause I'm rememberin' stuff —**

13   **rememberin' when I got busted for drunk driving.**

14   **Everybody says I was lucky not to get myself killed or kill**

15   **somebody else. And I know I was lucky 'cause the car was**

16   **totalled. So, for awhile I got smart and quit driving when I**

17   **was drinkin'.** *(Grins.)* **But I was still drinkin'. Y'know, man,**

18   **I mean — It helps you forget your problems. Well,** *(Shrugs)*

19   **helped me, anyhow. So, like I don't remember when I**

20   **started. I just know I'd drink anything in sight that had**

21   **alcohol in it, anytime I could find it. Which wasn't hard. Not**

22   **at my old man's place. Hell, it was easier to find his booze**

23   **than to find him. So anyhow, now I'm in one of those**

24   **counseling programs. You know, for** *(Makes quotation marks*

25   *in the air with his fingers)* **'Substance abusers.' I didn't think**

26   **alcohol counted as a 'substance.' I mean, we got pot heads**

27   **and speed freaks and you name it in our program. But my**

28   **counselors, I don't know, they consider alcohol a**

29   **substance, and me a substance abuser. Well, actually, my**

1 official title is an 'alcoholic.' Hey, at my age, I got a title
2 already. *(Shrugs)*
3   It's an okay program. I mean, if it can keep me from
4 windin' up like my old man, who's a real loser, then I'm
5 willin' to give it a try. For awhile, anyhow. You know, see
6 how it goes. I haven't had a drink this time around for three
7 months. Three months and sixteen days, to be exact. So,
8 no big deal, you say, huh? Well, for an 'alcoholic substance
9 abuser' it is a big deal, lemme tell ya. *(Nods, as if to himself)*
10 So, okay, why did I get started drinking in the first place? I
11 don't remember that. I mean, some things you remember,
12 and some things you don't. Right? I've thought about it, but
13 — well, there's this little story I really like. Says a lot, I
14 think. See, there's these two twins, and some dude says to
15 one of 'em, 'Hey, Joe, how come you drink?' And Joe says,
16 ' 'Cause my old man's an alcoholic.' And then this dude
17 asks the other twin, 'Hey, Moe, how come you don't drink?'
18 And Moe says, ' 'Cause my old man's an alcoholic.'
19 *(Chuckles)* Yeah, I like that one. *(Shrugs)* So, guess I'm the
20 first twin, huh? *(Shrugs and grins, snaps his finger a couple of*
21 *times and moves back into GROUP.)*
22
23
24
25
26
27
28
29
30
31
32
33
34
35

Adam and Eve's Diary
by Mark Twain

1 Eve — one day old   Female
2 Adam — age unspecified   Male
3
4   The final script for multiple voices features excerpts from Mark
5   Twain's separately published diaries of Adam and Eve. This
6   new adaptation alternates character lines of dialog to reveal
7   first impressions and final intimacies shared by Adam and
8   Eve. The script is appropriate for partner auditions, but may
9   also be edited as a solo monolog for either Adam or Eve. The
10   characters are human, and the obstacles they face are not
11   without moments of intrigue. Adam and Eve's witty and
12   sometimes wacky exchanges of dialog are always charming,
13   even when they're saying disagreeable things. In playing the
14   scene, you should remember that "what" is said and done is
15   not nearly as important as "how" it is said and done. So look
16   for the comic subtext in each character's vocal and physical
17   response.
18
19   *(Adam and Eve, peering out from behind flowering bushes in the*
20   *Garden of Eden, are surveying each other for the first time. First*
21   *sightings are not favorable. Each character furiously scribbles*
22   *notes in a diary, and the solemn air is punctuated at times with*
23   *loud grunts or soft groans to lend emphasis to the diary entry.*
24   *Against this colorful backdrop, Adam and Eve begin to peer*
25   *beneath the surface of outward appearances.)*
26
27 **EVE: Saturday. I am almost a whole day old now. I arrived**
28   **yesterday. It must be so, for it there was a day-before-**
29   **yesterday, I was not there when it happened; or I should**

1   remember it. It could be, of course, that it did happen and
2   I was not noticing. It will be best to start right now, and
3   not let the record get confused. For some instinct tells me
4   that these details are going to be important to the
5   historian some day.

6 ADAM: Monday. The new creature with the long hair is a good
7   deal in the way. It is always hanging around and following
8   me about. I am not used to company, and wish it would
9   stay with the other animals. Cloudy today. Think we shall
10   have rain ... We? Where did I get that word? I remember
11   now — the new creature uses it.

12 EVE: Tuesday. I followed the other Experiment around,
13   yesterday afternoon, to see what it might be for, if I could.
14   But I was not able to make it out. I think it is a man. I
15   have never seen a man, but it looked like one. It has
16   frowsy hair and blue eyes, and looks like a reptile. It has
17   no hips. It tapers like a carrot. When it stands, it spreads
18   itself apart like a derrick. Maybe it is architecture. I was
19   afraid of it at first, and started to run every time it turned
20   around. I thought it was going to chase me, but by-and-by
21   I found it was only trying to get away. So after that I was
22   not timid any more, but tracked it along, several hours,
23   about twenty yards behind. Which made it nervous and
24   unhappy. At last it was a good deal worried and climbed a
25   tree. I waited a while, then gave it up and went home.

26 ADAM: Sunday. This day is getting to be more and more
27   trying. It was selected and set apart as a day of rest. I
28   already had six of them per week, before. This morning
29   found the new creature trying to clod apples out of that
30   forbidden tree.

31 EVE: Tuesday. It is up in the tree again. Resting, apparently. It
32   looks to me like a creature that is more interested in
33   resting than in anything else. It has low tastes ... and is
34   not kind. It had crept down from the tree and was trying
35   to catch the little speckled fishes that play in the pool. I

1   had to clod it to make it go up the tree again and let them
2   alone. One of the clods took it back of the ear, and it used
3   language. I did not understand the words, but they
4   seemed expressive. When I found I could talk, I felt a new
5   interest in it. For I love to talk, all day, and in my sleep,
6   too. And I am very interesting. But if I had another to talk
7   to I could be twice as interesting, and would never stop.

8 ADAM: Wednesday. I wish it would not talk. It is always
9   talking right at my shoulder, right at my ear, and I am
10   used only to sounds that are more or less distant from
11   me. Been examining the great waterfall ... The new
12   creature calls it Niagara Falls — why, I am sure I do not
13   know. Says it looks like Niagara Falls. I get no chance to
14   name anything myself. The new creature names
15   everything that comes along, before I can get in a protest.
16   And always the same pretext is offered — it looks like the
17   thing. There is the dodo, for example. Says the moment
18   one looks at it one sees at a glance that it 'looks like a
19   Dodo.' It will have to keep that name, no doubt. Dodo! It
20   looks no more like a Dodo than I do!

21 EVE: Next Week Sunday. All week I tagged around after him
22   and tried to get more acquainted. I had to do the talking,
23   because he was shy. But I didn't mind. He seemed pleased
24   to have me around, and I used the sociable 'we' a good deal
25   because it seemed to flatter him to be included. He does
26   not try to avoid me as much, which is a good sign. During
27   the last day or two I have taken all the work of naming off
28   his hands for he has no gift in that line.

29 ADAM: Wednesday. Built me a shelter against the rain, but
30   could not have it to myself in peace. The new creature
31   intruded. When I tried to put it out, it shed water out of
32   the holes it looks with and wiped it away with the back of
33   its paws. And it made a noise such as some of the other
34   animals make when they are in distress. I wish it would
35   not talk so much! It is always talking. And the new

1   creature eats too much fruit. We are going to run short.

2   'We' again — that is its word. Mine, too, now from hearing

3   it so much.

4   EVE: Wednesday. I tried to get him some of those apples, but

5   I cannot learn to throw straight. I failed, but I think the

6   good intention pleased him. They are forbidden, and he

7   says I will come to harm.

8   ADAM: Thursday. It told me it was made out of a rib taken

9   from my body. This is at least doubtful, if not more than

10   that. I have not missed any rib ...

11 EVE: Monday. This morning I told him my name, hoping it

12   would interest him. But he did not care for it. It is strange.

13   If he should tell me his name, I would care.

14 ADAM: Monday. Its name is Eve. Says this word is to call it by

15   when I want it to come. Says it is not an It. It is a She.

16 EVE: Tuesday. He took no interest in my name. I tried to hide

17   my disappointment, but I suppose I did not succeed. I went

18   away and sat on the moss bank with my feet in the water.

19 ADAM: Sunday. Pulled through.

20 EVE: Tuesday. All morning I was at work improving the estate.

21   I purposely kept away from him in the hope that he would

22   get lonely and come. But he did not. I shall talk with the

23   snake. He is very kindly disposed ...

24 ADAM: Friday. She has taken up with a snake now. The other

25   animals are glad, for she is always experimenting with

26   them and bothering them. And I am glad because the

27   snake talks, and this enables me to get a rest. She is

28   always beseeching me to stop going over the falls. What

29   harm does it do? Says it makes her shudder. I wonder

30   why. I went over the falls in a barrel — not satisfactory to

31   her. Went over in a tub — still not satisfactory. Swam the

32   whirlpool and the rapids in a fig-leaf suit. It got much

33   damaged. I am too much hampered here. What I need is a

34   change of scene...

35 EVE: Sunday. It is pleasant again, now, and I am happy. But

1   those were heavy days. I do not think of them when I can
2   help it.
3 ADAM: Wednesday. I escaped last night and rode a horse all
4   night as fast as he could go. Hoping to clear out of the park
5   and hide in some other country before the trouble should
6   begin. But it was not to be. About an hour after sun-up, as
7   I was riding through a flowery plain where thousands of
8   animals were grazing, all of a sudden they broke into a
9   tempest of frightful noises. And in one moment the plain
10   was in a frantic commotion. And every beast was destroying
11   its neighbor. I knew what it meant — Eve had eaten that
12   fruit, and death was come into the world. I found this place,
13   outside the park, and was fairly comfortable for a few days.
14   But she found me out. I was not sorry she came, for there
15   are but meager pickings here. And she had brought me
16   some of those apples. I was obliged to eat them. I was so
17   hungry. She came curtained in boughs and bunches of
18   leaves. And when I snatched them away and asked her what
19   she meant by such nonsense, she tittered and blushed. She
20   said I myself would soon know why it was thus. This was
21   correct. I laid down the apple, half-eaten — certainly the
22   best one I ever saw, considering the lateness of the season
23   — and arrayed myself in the discarded boughs and
24   branches. I ordered her to go and get some more and not to
25   make a spectacle of herself. Afterward, we crept down to
26   where the wild-beast battle had been, and collected some
27   skins. I made her patch together a couple of different suits
28   proper for public presentation. They are uncomfortable, it is
29   true, but stylish. And that is the main point about clothes.
30   I find she is a good deal of a companion. I see I should be
31   lonesome and depressed without her. Another thing, she
32   says it is ordered that we work for our living hereafter. She
33   will be useful. I will supervise.
34 EVE: Friday. I tried once more to persuade him to stop going
35   over the falls. That was because the fire which I had

1   discovered had revealed to me a new passion. Quite new,
2   and distinctly different from love, grief, and those others
3   which I had already discovered — fear.
4 ADAM: Friday. Perhaps I ought to remember that she is a very
5   young girl and make allowances. She is all interest,
6   eagerness, vivacity. And the world is to her a charm, a
7   wonder, a mystery, a joy. And she is color-mad! Brown
8   rocks, yellow sand, gray moss, green foliage, blue sky, the
9   pearl of the dawn — none of them is of any practical value,
10   as far as I can see. But because they have color and
11   majesty that is enough for her, and she loses her mind
12   over them. If she could but quiet down and keep still a
13   couple minutes at a time, I think I could enjoy looking at
14   her. Indeed, I am sure I could. Once, when she was
15   standing marble-white and sun-drenched on a boulder,
16   with her head tilted back and her hand shading her eyes,
17   I recognized that she was beautiful.
18 EVE: Friday, Six Months Later. Tuesday — Wednesday —
19   Thursday — and today — all without seeing him. It is a
20   long time to be alone. But he will come back soon.
21 ADAM: Next Year. Monday. We have named it Cain. She caught
22   it while I was away trapping on the North Shore of the Erie.
23   It resembles us in some ways, and may be a close relation.
24   That is what she thinks, but this is an error, in my
25   judgment. The difference in size warrants that it is a
26   different and new kind of animal — a fish, perhaps. Though
27   when I put it in the water to see, it sank. And she plunged
28   in and snatched it out before there was an opportunity for
29   me to determine the matter. Wednesday. It isn't a fish. It
30   makes curious noises when not satisfied, and says 'goo
31   goo' when it is. It is not one of us, for it doesn't walk. Three
32   Months Later. I sleep but little. It has ceased lying around,
33   and goes about on its four legs now. Yet it differs from the
34   other four-legged animals in that its front legs are
35   unusually short. This causes the main part of the animal to

1   stick up, uncomfortably high in the air, and this is not
2   attractive. Three Months Later. The Kangaroo still
3   continues to grow. It has fur on its head now; except that
4   it is much finer and softer. And instead of being black it's
5   red. Five Months Later. The Bear has learned to paddle
6   around all by itself on its hind legs, and says 'poppa' and
7   'momma.' It is certainly a new species. I will go off on a far
8   expedition among the forests of the north and make an
9   exhaustive search. There must certainly be another one
10   somewhere, and this one will be less dangerous when it
11   has company of its own species. In my judgment, it is
12   either an enigma or some kind of bug.

13   Three Months Later. It has been a weary hunt, and I
14   have had no success. In the meantime, without stirring
15   from the home estate she has caught another one! I never
16   saw such luck! This new one is as ugly now as the old one
17   was at first. It has the same sulphur and raw meat
18   complexion and the same singular head without any fur
19   on it ... She calls it Abel. Ten Years Later. They are boys!
20   We found it out long ago. It was their coming in that small
21   shape that puzzled us. There are some girls now too. Abel
22   is a good boy, but if Cain had stayed a bear it would have
23   improved him.

24   EVE: Five Years Later. After the Fall. When I look back, the
25   Garden is a dream. It was beautiful, enchantingly
26   beautiful. And now it is lost. And I shall not see it any
27   more. The garden is lost, but I have him. He loves me as
28   well as he can. I love him with all the strength of my
29   passionate nature. If I ask myself why I love him, I find I
30   do not know. I love certain birds because of their song.
31   But I do not love Adam on account of his singing — no, it
32   is not that! The more he sings, the more I do not get
33   reconciled to it. It is not on account of his gracious and
34   considerate ways and his delicacy that I love him. No, he
35   has lacks in these regards. But he is well enough, and is

1   improving. It is not on account of his chivalry that I love
2   him — no, it is not that. He told on me, but I do not blame
3   him. It is a peculiarity of his sex, I think. And he did not
4   make his sex. Of course, I would not have told on him. I
5   would have perished first. But that is a peculiarity of my
6   sex. And I do not take credit for it, for I did not make my
7   sex. Then why is it that I love him? He is strong and
8   handsome, but I could love him without those qualities. If
9   he were plain, I should love him. And I would work for him,
10   slave over him, pray for him, and watch by his bedside
11   until I died. I think I love him merely because he is mine.
12   There is no other reason, I suppose. It just comes — and
13   cannot explain itself. And it does not need to.
14   ADAM: Ten Years Later. After all these years, I see that I was
15   mistaken about Eve in the beginning. It is better to live
16   outside the Garden with her than inside it without her. At
17   first, I thought she talked too much. But now I should be
18   sorry to have that voice fall silent and pass out of my life.
19   Blessed be the one that brought us together and taught
20   me to know the goodness of her heart and the sweetness
21   of her spirit.
22   EVE: Forty Years Later. It is my longing, it is my prayer, that
23   we may pass from this life together. A longing which shall
24   never perish from the earth, but shall have a place in the
25   heart of every wife that loves, until the end of time. And it
26   shall be called by my name. But if one of us must go first,
27   it is my prayer that it shall be I. For life without him would
28   not be life. How could I endure it? This prayer is also
29   immortal, and will not cease from being offered up while
30   my race continues. I am the first wife, and in the last wife
31   I shall be repeated.
32   ADAM: At Eve's Grave. Wheresoever she was, there was Eden.
33
34
35

Legal Acknowledgments

Copyright Caution

Copyright laws exist to protect the artistic and intellectual property rights of creators of original works. All creative works like scripts are considered copyrighted. There are, however, a number of "fair use" exceptions for educational or instructional purposes related to classroom performance. The scripts in this volume are fully protected under the copyright laws of the United States, the British Empire, the Dominion of Canada, and all other countries of the Copyright Union. For additional information related to full-scale productions or other available scripts please contact the author or the author's agent at the address listed.

Voices of Hope and Longing

The Last Yankee by Arthur Miller. Copyright © 1997 by Arthur Miller. Reprinted by permission of International Creative Management, Inc. For additional information please contact the author's agent at International Creative Management, 40 West 57th Street, New York, New York 10019.

I Hate Hamlet by Paul Rudnick. Copyright © 1992 by Paul Rudnick. Reprinted by permission of Dramatists Play Service, Inc. The English language stock and amateur stage performance rights are controlled exclusively by Dramatists Play Service, Inc., 440 Park Avenue South, New York, New York 10016. No professional or nonprofessional performance of the play may be given without obtaining, in advance, the written permission of Dramatists Play Service, Inc., and paying the requisite fee. Inquiries concerning all other rights should be addressed to Helen Merrill Ltd., 295 Lafayette Street, Suite 915, New York, New York 10012.

A Flower or Something by Jolene Goldenthal. Copyright © 2001 by Jolene Goldenthal. All rights reserved. Reprinted by permission of the author and Susan Schulman, A Literary Agency. For additional information please contact Susan Schulman, A Literary Agency, 454 West 44th Street, New York, New York 10036.

Trophies by John J. Wooten. Copyright © 1994 by John J. Wooten. Reprinted by permission of the author. For additional information please contact Ron Gwiazda at Rosenstone/Wender, 38 East 29th Street, 10th Floor, New York, New York 10016 or the author at wootenj@mail.montclair.edu.

The Innocents Crusade by Keith Reddin. Copyright © 1993 by Keith Reddin. Reprinted by permission of Dramatists Play Service, Inc. The English language stock and amateur stage performance rights are controlled exclusively by Dramatists Play Service Inc., 440 Park Avenue South, New York, New York 10016. No professional or nonprofessional performance of the play may be given without obtaining, in advance, the written permission of Dramatists Play Service, Inc., and paying the requisite fee. Inquiries concerning all other rights should be addressed to the William Morris Agency, Inc., 1325 Avenue of the Americas, New York, New York 10019.

Women Behind the Walls by Claire Braz-Valentine. Copyright © 2001 by Claire Braz-Valentine. Reprinted by permission of the author. For additional information please contact the author at cbrazvalen@aol.com.

251

Voices of Spirit and Soul

the author at New Dramatists, 424 West 44th Street, New York, New York 10036.

Spirit Awakening by Akuyoe Graham. Copyright © 2000 by Akuyoe Graham. Reprinted by permission of Spirit Awakening Foundation. For additional information please contact Spirit Awakening Foundation, 2300 Westwood Boulevard, Suite 106, Los Angeles, California 90064.

New York Trucker by Alison Rosenfeld-Desmarais. Copyright © 2000 by Alison Rosenfeld-Desmarais. Reprinted by permission of the author. For additional information please contact the author c/o Peter Giagni, 8981 Sunset Boulevard, Suite 103, West Hollywood, California 90069.

Eating Out by Marcia Dixcy. Copyright © 2000 by Marcia Dixcy. Reprinted by permission of the author. For additional information please contact the author at dixcyjory@aol.com.

Death Comes to Us All, Mary Agnes by Christopher Durang. Copyright © 1980, 1982, 1995 by Christopher Durang. Reprinted by permission of Helen Merrill, Ltd. and Dramatists Play Service, Inc. The stage performance rights in this play are controlled exclusively by Dramatists Play Service, Inc., 440 Park Avenue South, New York, New York 10016. No professional or nonprofessional performance of the play may be given without obtaining, in advance, the written permission of Dramatists Play Service, Inc., and paying the requisite fee. Inquiries concerning all other rights should be addressed to the author's agent c/o Helen Merrill Ltd., 295 Lafayette Street, Suite 915, New York, New York 10012.

Stepping Out by Richard Harris. Copyright © 1985, 1995 by Richard Harris. Reprinted by permission of The Agency (London) Ltd. First published by Amber Lane Press. For additional information please contact The Agency (London) Ltd., 24 Pottery Lane, London W 11, 4 LZ England.

Amara by Leigh Podgorski. Copyright © 1995 by Leigh Podgorski. Reprinted by permission of the author. For additional information please contact the author at 17139 Cantara Street, Van Nuys, California 91406 or leighpod@aol.com.

A Woman Called Truth by Sandra Fenichel Asher. Copyright © 1993 by Sandra Fenichel Asher. Reprinted by permission of Dramatic Publishing. All rights reserved. For additional information please contact the publisher at 311 Washington Street, Woodstock, Illinois 60098.

Happy Birthday, Dad by Don P. Norman. Copyright © 1998 by Don P. Norman. Reprinted by permission of the author. For additional information please contact the author at 900 N. Randolph Street, #201, Arlington, Virginia 22203 or at dcscribe@netbox.com.

Two Minutes Too Long by Colin Donald. Copyright © 1995 by Colin Donald. Reprinted by permission of the author. For additional information please contact the author at 549 Canning Street, Carlton North, Victoria 3054, Australia.

Voices of Fantasy and Fun

Little Red Riding Hood's Mother by Tammy Ryan. Copyright © 2000 by Tammy

The Indelicate Instructor by Rev. Jay Goldstein. Copyright © 1999 by Rev. Jay Goldstein. Reprinted by permission of the author. For additional information please contact the author at jay@jaygoldstein.net.

Men & Cars by Diane Spodarek. Copyright © 1993 by Diane Spodarek. Reprinted by permission of the author. For additional information please contact the author at 385 Grand Street, #L1508, New York, New York 10002 or at dianedetroit@aol.com.

The Fastest Clock in the Universe by Philip Ridley. Copyright © 1999 by Philip Ridley. Reprinted by permission of the author and Methuen Publishing Limited (Ridley Plays 1). For additional information please contact the publisher at 215 Vauxhall Bridge Road, London SW1V, 1EJ, England.

Tea by Velina Hasu Houston. Copyright © 1987 by Velina Hasu Houston. Reprinted by permission of the author and Harden-Curtis Associates. All rights, including professional and amateur stage rights, motion picture, recitation, lecturing, public reading, radio broadcasting, television, video or sound recording, all other forms of mechanical or electronic reproduction, such as CD-ROM, CD-1, information storage and retrieval systems and photocopying, and the rights of translation into foreign languages, are strictly reserved. Particular emphasis is placed upon the matter of readings, permission for which must be secured from the Author's agent in writing. Inquiries concerning all other rights should be addressed to Mary Harden c/o Harden-Curtis Associates, 850 Seventh Avenue, Suite 903, New York, New York 10019.

The Madness of Esme and Shaz by Sarah Daniels. Copyright © 1999 by Sarah Daniels. Reprinted by permission of the author and Methuen Publishing Limited (Daniels Plays 2). For additional information please contact the publisher at 215 Vauxhall Bridge Road, London SW1V, 1EJ, England.

Once a Catholic by Mary O'Malley. Copyright © 1988 by Mary O'Malley. Reprinted by permission of Amber Lane Press, Ltd. For additional information please contact the publisher at Church Street, Charlbury, Oxford OX7, 3PR, England.

Class Action by Brad Slaight. Copyright © 1996 by Brad Slaight. Reprinted by permission of Baker's Plays, Inc. For additional information please contact the publisher at P.O. Box 699222, Quincy, Massachusetts 02269 or call (617) 745-0805.

In Poetic Defence by Richard Gilbert Hill. Copyright © 2000 by Richard Gilbert Hill. Reprinted by permission of the author. For additional information please contact the author at 150 N. Beachwood Drive, Apt. #C, Burbank, California 91506. You may also review other scripts by contacting the author at richardhill@themonologueshop.com.

Medea by Christopher Durang and Wendy Wasserstein. Copyright © 1998 by Christopher Durang and Wendy Wasserstein. Reprinted by permission of Helen Merrill Ltd. and Dramatists Play Service. The stage performance rights in this play are controlled exclusively by Dramatists Play Service, Inc., 440 Park Avenue South, New York, New York 10016. No professional or nonprofessional performance of the play may be given without obtaining, in advance, the written permission of Dramatists Play Service, Inc., and paying the requisite fee. Inquiries concerning all other rights should be addressed to the author's agent c/o Helen Merrill Ltd., 295 Lafayette Street, Suite 915, New York, New York 10012.

Voices of Despair and Doubt